THE GOAT

THE QUEST
TO FIND THE BEST

THE TOP 75
BASKETBALL
PLAYERS OF
ALL TIME

The G.O.A.T – The Quest to Find the Best
The Top 75 Basketball Players of All Time – 2022 Edition
Copyright © 2022 by Jack L. Sutter

First Edition Published in 2022

ISBN-13: 979-8-218-21564-4

Library of Congress Cataloging-in-Publication Data

Library of Congress Registration
Sutter, Jack L.
The G.O.A.T – The Quest to Find the Best
Registration Number: TXu 2-338-191 | October 2023

Category: Basketball Players, Sports, Basketball

Written by: Jack L. Sutter | jackomaxo1@gmail.com

Edited by: Amy Crosby & Ashlee Predmore

Cover Design Formatting by: Eli Blyden Sr. | www.EliTheBookGuy.com

Formatting Assisted by: Jahshua Blyden

Printed in the USA by: A&A Printing & Publishing | www.PrintShopCentral.com

To my wife of over 50 years, Diane,
for her encouragement and faith in me.

TABLE OF CONTENTS

THE QUEST TO RECOGNIZE THE BEST

One of the most talked about and debated subjects in all of sports, especially within the football community, is who is the G.O.A.T. The acronym (Greatest of All Time) used and made popular most recently with the announced retirement of Tom Brady. (Brady decided to unretire, but the talk is ongoing about Brady being the greatest football player of all time.) Brady has elevated the G.O.A.T. talk to unparalleled levels by fans and sports personalities alike. There are even commercials based on the G.O.A.T. theme. Is Tom Brady the best player to EVER play in the National Football League? Many fans would say that he is the greatest, but based on what? His teams have won seven Super Bowls so based on that; he probably is the greatest. Brady is also entering an unprecedented twenty-third year in the NFL, which is the longest by a non-special teams' player in the history of the league. His longevity would add credibility to his ranking for sure. However, Brady is the first to acknowledge that football is a team game. No one person no matter how great can win a game or certainly not a Super Bowl.

The term greatest of all time, The G.O.A.T., has morphed into discussions on sports talk radio, sports publications and among sports fans about who is the best to ever play in other sports as well. In the sport of baseball, Babe Ruth is probably most often mentioned as the greatest to ever play baseball. In the sport of hockey, Wayne Gretzky is considered by most hockey fans to be the G.O.A.T. So how about basketball? Several sports talk personalities as well as the NBA itself has published their picks for the All-Time NBA team, a Top 75. Picking just ONE of those seventy-five players is much more difficult and much more controversial. An argument can be made for anyone of perhaps a half dozen players. Every sports fan likes to debate and discuss who the G.O.A.T. is in each sport. Who are the athletes who would have their faces etched on Mt. Rushmore as the greatest of all time in their respective sports? Sports fans have an opinion about almost anything that has to do with their sport. That's why they are called fans, short for fanatics. An opinion is defined as a view or judgement. Some opinions are based solely on a feeling or a prejudice, some are based on statistics, some on experience, and some are based on sound established concepts. However, the greatest of all time in any sport boils down to just a person's opinion. It is not a science or a provable theory, it's a subjective point of view. What makes one person's opinion carry more "weight" than another? Why do some people pay more attention to what one person thinks as opposed to another? Most sports fans put more credibility in the opinion of a sports commentator, sportswriter, a sports network, a former player or a person that has "firsthand" knowledge such as a coach or former player. But while that might give more credibility to that person's opinion, does that make their opinion right? Of course not. In every subjective opinion or view a person's bias and prejudice creeps into the thought process. That is called being a human not a robot. So how is the true G.O.A.T. chosen and is it even possible to pick just the one greatest? The honest answer to that question is it's impossible. It is a subjective, complicated, and very unscientific process that can only be narrowed down to a person's choice. However, I do think it is possible to establish a set of criteria that can help one make an "educated choice". It is possible to elevate the debate on who is the greatest of all time in any sport to a level of sanity beyond just a group of fanatics sitting in a bar or a panel of so-called sports gurus arguing their point of view.

I have tried to make an argument for how difficult it truly is to pick the one greatest in any sport. Picking the one most elite is an impossibility! But as a fan it is fun and entertaining to try. I understand that some opinions carry more credibility than others due to experiences, knowledge, or perhaps association. That does not make that person's view right but with a sound criterion it may make that person's opinion carry more weight or more credible. As a former Illinois All-State high school basketball player, a coach for over 20 years at the high school, junior college, and college level I think I bring a unique prospective to the debate. I have also been a fan for seven decades and have had the privilege of SEEING practically every one of the 4374 players who have played in the NBA. I was born two years before the league was formed. While it may be true that I have no "firsthand" experience from either playing or coaching in the NBA, I would argue that neither has 95% of those sports personalities that claim to be an authority. I have coached several great college players and a few of them have gone on to play in the NBA. I have also played against a few players during my playing days at Middle Tennessee State University who ended up having good careers in the NBA. I can tell you unequivocally that those players were extremely talented. But the basketball players that play at a "rarefied level," those that I rate as the Top 75 of all time are generational.

That brings me back to the G.O.A.T. discussion. In my opinion I do not think it is possible or fair to so many great basketball players that have played in the NBA to pick just ONE greatest of all time. I believe it is possible to narrow the possibilities if we change the focus and the acronym from the greatest of ALL time to the greatest of A time. It is impossible to compare athletes and their accomplishments fairly and equitably from one generation to another. The game has changed, the rules have changed, even the court has changed. In my seven decades of watching basketball, I have witnessed a lot of changes to the game, including the level of skill exhibited by the players. Could some of the greatest players such as George Miken or Bob Cousy of the 40s and 50s play in the NBA today? Absolutely! I have broken my selections down by decades and I'm sure there will be a lot of fans that will not agree with all my picks. I think by picking the All-Decade teams the 4374 who have played in the NBA are reduced to a more "manageable" 100 legitimate contenders. While I think it is impossible to pick just one player that is the G.O.A.T., I intend to try. I have spent the last several months analyzing, looking at volumes of statistics, and trying to figure it out.

CHOICES BASED ON SOUND CRITERIA

I have chosen these 75 players for my all-time NBA team based on a set criterion that I think is sound and has merit. I have pinned my criteria here for each reader to see and to be able to refer to as you go through the player's bios. In some cases, it is a little more complicated than just following a set of guidelines, but I will do my best to follow my "own rules." I think by establishing and following a defined criteria it helps to eliminate prejudices which is one of the greatest obstacles to compiling such an elite list. I have tried to be as open minded and as objective as humanly possible. A definitive criterion provides a solid foundation for these choices, and I believe that my criteria is very comprehensive. I understand this is only one man's opinion. Of course, I have my all-time "favorites," some of them made the list and some did not. I could not prove in a court of law or by any scientific equation that my picks are the right picks. My intention is not to convince any NBA fan that I am right, or my picks are better than theirs. I want to acknowledge that several of my picks are the result of my experiences in just being around the game of basketball and watching these players perform. I refer to this as the "eye test." As a player and later as a coach I have participated in the sport of basketball for over 35 years. I believe that I have a unique perspective and understand the game well enough to make definable and defensible choices based on these solid criteria. I have the utmost respect for anyone who has ever played in the NBA, each one is an exceptional athlete.

I have made my picks of the Top 75 based on ten factors that as a coach I used to evaluate players to award scholarships and to "game plan" when my teams played against great players.

1-DOMINANCE

The #1 criteria that I think trumps all the others is dominance. What do I mean by dominance? I do not believe that a player can make the all-time best 75 players in the history of the NBA if they were not dominant in their own era. To be considered as one of the best to ever play the game that player had to be the best player on the court every time he stepped on it. He also had to be the best player in the conference or league in the era that he played. It is difficult to pick the very best of the best. However, there is always something that gives one player the edge over another, even at the highest level. I go back to the statement that I made earlier about how difficult it is to name the greatest of "ALL" time as opposed to the greatest of "A" time. It is very difficult, if not impossible, to compare a player from the 60s or 70s to a player today. But it is not hard to recognize greatness! It is also very hard to compare the skills of a point guard with the skills of a center. Who dominated the game? I have seen a game taken over by a guard and by a center. Every player I chose in my Top 75 dominated their era. The criteria or guidelines that I intend to use to support my all-time Top 75 NBA team, as well as my All-Decade teams, are vital to making this whole process fair and equitable.

I have enjoyed this great game of basketball since I was about eight years old and began playing on an outdoor dirt court. As a player and a coach, those players that totally dominated the game both on the offensive and defensive end of the court are still vivid to me. They are the players that as a fan you remember for a lifetime. Like a historical event, you remember where you were when you saw them play, and certainly what it was like to play against them. It was truly memorable. My first encounter with such a player was as a sophomore in high school when we played against McLeansboro High School. They had the second-best high school player in the state of Illinois, Jerry Sloan. Sloan played at a level that very few high school players ever rise to. He scored 35 points against us and didn't even play the last quarter. He was DOMINANT. He went on to be an All-American in college at Evansville University after he transferred from the University of Illinois. He was an outstanding pro with the Chicago Bulls, where he made several All-Defensive teams. He recently was voted one of the 15 best coaches in the history of the NBA.

Another example of dominance that comes to mind was a Big Ten game I attended as a sophomore in high school. Every winter, my family went to visit some friends that lived in Champaign, Il (about a two-hour drive from our home in Galatia, Il). We always planned our trips so we could attend a Big Ten game at the University of Illinois. I loved the Big 10 and looked forward to watching the "game of the week" every Saturday afternoon on TV. In 1960 our friends got us tickets to see the Illini play Ohio State. That Buckeye team had Jerry Lucas, John Havlicek, Mel Nowell, Larry Siegfried, and Joe Roberts. (Bob Knight was a substitute on that team.) It was the greatest college team I had ever seen, and still ranks in my top 10 of all time. I sat there in the bleachers thinking how great it would be to be that good and to play on a team that good. That team went on to win the National Championship. I still remember that like it was last week, truly memorable. As a player in college, I had the misfortune of playing against and trying to guard a dominant player from Western Kentucky University by the name of Clem Haskins. Haskins was player of the year in the Ohio Valley Conference all three years he played for the Hilltoppers. He was a college All-American and a first-round draft pick of the Chicago Bulls. He went on to play nine years for three teams in the NBA and finished with a career average of 12.8 points. He was DOMINANT.

As a high school coach in Florida for nine years we played against several D1 players but one of those players was head and shoulders above the others. My team played in a summer league that had a team from Auburndale, Florida. That team had a junior player by the name of Tracy

McGrady. McGrady didn't even warm up before the game, he just strolled into the gym and threw up 30 points in the FIRST HALF. We were down by 20 at half time. We had a guard that signed at a D1 school that year, but he still made all my players look like grade school players. I said at the time he could be playing in college right then. McGrady went straight to the NBA out of prep school a year later. He was DOMINANT.

As an assistant coach at Oral Roberts University for four years I saw dominating play from our players and from opposing players. I could site several examples but the one that stands out in my mind was a skinny kid I remembered playing at a high school near where I grew up in Southern Illinois. Doug Collins went from a good 6'2" high school guard at Benton, Il. to a 6'6" All-American at Illinois State University. Our ORU team played ISU every year I was at ORU and while we never lost to them Collins scored 30 or more points every game. We could not guard him. Fortunately, we had our own dominant player in Richard Fuqua. Collins went on to play in the NBA for 8 years, made the all-star team 4 times and played in the 1972 Olympics. He was a DOMINANT player. Richard Fuqua was a 6'3" guard for us that finished second in the nation in scoring one year and third another. He averaged over 30 points a game. Richard became the first All-American to play at ORU. He scored 44 points in the first round of the NIT against Memphis State the first time we played there in 1971. He could reel off 10 points in a matter of minutes, and that was before the three-point line. He was unstoppable, DOMINANT. These kinds of players could take over a game and beat you by themselves. My last year as an assistant at ORU in 1974 we played Kansas in the finals of the Mid-West Regional for a chance to go to the Final Four. Two nights before the Kansas game we played Louisville who had an All-American and NBA player named Junior Bridgeman. Bridgeman played in the NBA for 12 years and averaged 13 points for his career. He was a great player who could DOMINATE a game.

Domination happens at every level of competition whether it is in high school, college, or at the professional level. Every athlete rises to a level that is their "maximum level of success," their potential. For most athletes it is high school, for maybe 5 to 7 percent of all high school players it is Division 1, and for the best of the best (maybe 1 percent of the athletes at D 1 schools) get an opportunity to play for pay. Of those in that 1 percentile, even they get dominated by the players that are written about in this book!

2-LONGEVITY

My second pillar in picking the best of the best is longevity. I would like to use a baseball analogy to make my point. One of my most favorite baseball players of all time is Sandy Koufax who pitched for the Dodgers from 1955 to 1966. During those 11 years he won 3 Cy Youngs, 2 World Series MVPs, he was 5 times ERA leader, pitched 4 no hitters, made the all-star team 7 times and won 165 games, twice as many as he lost. He was a first ballot (87%) Hall of Famer. Those are some unbelievable stats and accomplishments for the eleven years he played and for 7 years he dominated. He was truly a great pitcher in his era, a great pitcher in every sense of the word. But I would not pick Koufax as my baseball G.O.A.T. There are other pitchers who put up those kinds of numbers over a longer period. I would rate them ahead of Koufax as my pick for the greatest of ALL time. For almost a decade he was the greatest! But as great as Koufax was his domination did not last as long as several other great pitchers who pitched in the major leagues. While dominance is my #1 criteria it is not my only criteria. Most fans, I think would agree with me, that another important mark of greatness is longevity. I think it is important to perform at a high level over an extended period. A player that gives the same high level of performance night after night, and year after year. I also believe it is more difficult to remain on top than it is to get to the top. Maybe not a Tom Brady type career but a career that is measured by "years" of excellence. The so called "one and done" players are not on this list. There are some great players that did not make my Top 75 because their careers were not long enough due to injuries. For whatever reason they just couldn't stay healthy. I intend to recognize these players in a "special mention" section later in this book.

I reward consistency and appreciate the dedication, hard work, commitment and sometimes the good fortune that it takes to stay healthy for a long time. As a coach I was always looking for consistency in my players throughout the season. There is a saying in the coaching world that "he (player) is just good enough to get you fired" meaning you can never depend on the player competing at a high level from game to game. Everyone sees the potential and the possibilities of what that player can do, but as a coach you can't count on that "showing up" every night. Multiply that by years and the importance of consistency and longevity becomes even more significant. Basketball is a demanding game on one's body and to stay healthy demands a very high level of commitment and discipline. I understand that some athletes, through no choice of their own and despite all they did to stay healthy, seemed to just be prone to injuries. Bill Walton is a perfect example of that, and I will talk about him later.

Before I get into the rest of my criteria, I need to pause here and make a distinction between the greatest and the most valuable. This is a book about those players I consider the elite of the elite. A player can be of immeasurable importance to the success of a team while not being great. In other words, a KEY player to a team winning a championship by fulfilling a particular ROLE on a team such as an outstanding rebounder and/or defensive player. That doesn't mean the role player is not important it does mean he is not "the man", he is not the player that the opposition has to "game scheme" for. He is never the BEST player on his team or on the court. There is a player that has made almost everyone's Top 75 based on being a great rebounder and defensive player. He also played on several championship teams but always with other great players. One of those players many NBA fans consider to be the G.O.A.T. This player was never the best or even second-best player on any of the teams that won the championships. He averaged less than seven points a game in the play-offs and about 10 rebounds. He made the All-Defensive team 8 times which is a great accomplishment to be sure. Rebounding is important and holding an offensive player below his scoring average contributes to a winning team, but it does not make a player elite. Is a player like that valuable, of course, but in coaching we refer to that player as being a significant ROLE player? A player like that is critical to building a championship team but could you win a championship with that player being your best player? Probably not. While any coach, including me, would like to have a player who plays as hard and is as competitive as Dennis Rodman he does not meet my criteria for greatness.

3-OFFENSE vs. DEFENSE

Defense win's championships, so THEY say, but I have never seen a contest of any kind won by not scoring. The object of the game is to score more points than your opponent. I told my son and my grandsons when they began to play basketball that they had to learn to shoot the ball and learn to shoot it correctly because unless they grew to be 6'10" they would never get to play at a high level if they could not score. Every coach is looking for someone who can score the basketball. Offense is harder to master than defense. Offense requires skill, defense requires determination. I'm not making these statements to criticize defense in any way I know from coaching for over 20 years that teams that play good, solid defense are usually successful. I also know that defense shows up every night and is a more consistent facet of the game than offense. I am simply saying it takes more skill and talent to shoot a basketball that to stop someone from shooting a basketball. I have never driven by an outdoor court and seen boys practicing defense and working on their "slides." As a coach I never prepared my team to focus on the best defensive player on the other team, but I have spent a lot of time and game planning on stopping the opponent's best scorer. Who does the coach want the ball in the hands of when the game is on the line? Offensive players are special talents which is why I place such importance on offense in selecting my Top 75.

4-PHYSICALITY

The fourth criteria that I have based my picks for the elite list is physicality. Physicality as defined by Webster as an "intensely physical orientation." God didn't make us all equal in respect to our physical makeup. Size, quickness or jumping ability does not guarantee someone will be an exceptional basketball player. But it does guarantee that that person, with work, skill and determination has a much better chance of being an elite athlete than one who does not have that exceptional body. Of course, a basketball player that is not physically gifted can play at a high level but usually that level is not in the NBA. I do not have the time or space here to list all the truly great college players that didn't make it in the NBA because they were "out sized" and over matched in the NBA. As a former player, a little point guard of 6'1", I am proud to honestly and unashamedly list some "smaller" basketball GIANTS in my Top 75. They are truly special in many ways. They overcame a tremendous barrier to excel. NBA players are some of the most physically gifted athletes in the world but that alone is not enough to make the list. It is those that are specially gifted physically that take their game to another level thru hard work, dedication, determination and the drive to be the best that sets them apart. There are also the intangibles that drive them to be the best especially in the most crucial game situations. The greatest players believe that they can make the basket, make a stop, get a rebound, and win the game. Most everyone that has followed the NBA for any amount of time would concede that the NBA players today are bigger, stronger, quicker and can jump higher than at any other time in the history of the league.

Some NBA followers might even believe some of the great players of the early years of the league could not play in the modern NBA. I believe that many players who played 30 years ago would still be exceptional players today. There is no question that the game has seen its ebbs and flows regarding the physicality of play. I think that even though the players today may be bigger and quicker they also enjoy the benefit of the way the game is officiated. I agree with former great Rick Barry that thinks players today walk or travel on almost every possession, thus gaining an advantage. How much would a player like Pete Maravich benefit from how loosely the referees call traveling in the NBA today? I think the game has gotten much more physical as well. Basketball was once described as a game of finesse, "a ballet" performed in sneakers. Now, I would describe the sport as hockey played in sneakers. But does that mean that some of the greats of the early years of the league could not play and excel against today's players? Not at all, they would adjust their game. I think several players from 50 years ago are just as exceptional as those who are playing today. There weren't any 6'9" guards in the early days of the NBA but keep in mind that comparing players from one generation to another is not fair or even possible. It is generational and players of the early days of the NBA were just as exceptional as the players of the 2000s. The better question is, who were the dominant players in the time period that they played?

5-STATISTICS

"Figures don't lie but liars do figures." That may be an "old" saying but it is true. For purposes here, I would change that to statistics don't lie but they can be used to promote or support a biased argument. There is no question that a player's stats play a significant role in defining that player's accomplishments and their rank among their peers. However, it becomes more difficult when stats of one era are compared with the players stats in another era. The number of games played, the changes in the court such as a wider lane, the shot clock, a 3-point line, etc. alters the significance of the statistics. Other important factors that influence a player's personal statistics is whether the player played on a great team with other great players and what position the player played. Does a player's average (points, rebounds, assist, etc.) go up during playoffs or down? Each of these variables must be considered when recognizing just how great a player is. They also give some insight into whether that player is a "clutch" player or not. I will discuss and define clutch in greater detail later. The position the player plays is a major factor into such things as field goal percentage, rebounds, and assists. Without question the 3-point arc has changed the game more than any other one thing that I can think of. An asterisk must be included in the scoring statistics of all players who played before the 1979-80 season when the 3-point shot went into effect. As a coach I even changed my offensive scheme from running a fastbreak with the wing players cutting to the basket to the wing players flaring to the corners for the three. I think it has been great for the game to open up the court especially since the players are much bigger. It has afforded the "little man" an opportunity to make just as big an impact on the outcome of the game as the "big man". Stephen Curry is now getting mentioned by many sports media personalities as perhaps a top ten player because of the 3-pointer and his impact on the game.

Statistics while very important are only one of my ten criteria. Some statistical categories have been added that were not a part of the early years of basketball. For example, Bill Russell is generally recognized as the best defensive center to ever play in the NBA because of his ability to block shots. (Russell passed away just a about a month before this book went to the printer.) His Celtic teams won 11 World Championships. Even though the NBA did not keep track of blocked shots during most of Russell's career he is still recognized as one of the best of all-time. (The NBA began keeping the stats for blocked shots in 1973-74.) In the modern era Hakeem Olajuwon, Dikembe Mutombo and Kareem Abdul-Jabbar are the top three shot blockers. However, there is also a record of 112 games that Wilt Chamberlain played in where he averaged 8.8 blocks per game. All five of these centers were intimidators and great shot blockers but if that stat would have been kept for Chamberlain's entire career, he could have averaged over 10 blocks a game and recorded a triple-double for his career. Wilt would have been the all-time shot blocker not Olajuwon. He was already 35 years old and in the twilight of his career in 1974 when the NBA began recording blocks. I had the privilege of seeing both Chamberlain and Russell play and they pass the "eye test" when it comes to being great shot blockers. The era in which the stats were being recorded must be kept in context. When analyzing the greatest players in NBA history this simple concept is frequently not considered. Raw numbers (statistics) can be deceiving when not viewed in their proper context.

Perhaps nothing has impacted NBA statistics and records as much as the 3-point arc. As mentioned earlier, the 3-point field goal has altered how the game is played and changed the impact that outside scoring has on the modern game. Guards have more influence now than at any point in the history of the game from a scoring standpoint. I'll discuss this more in detail later in the book.

A final point to be made about statistics is that on a team that is "loaded" with offensive players, such as the great Lakers or Celtics teams, several great players might not put up the "numbers" that a great player on a poor team might record. How many shots and how many points will a 3rd or 4th option player get? James Worthy is a great offensive player who played on the same team as Magic Johnson and Kareem Abdul-Jabbar in the 80s. Worthy was not the "go to" guy on a team like that. Ray Allen is another example of a great offensive player that "sacrificed" his numbers during his five years with the Celtics. He played with Kevin Garnett and Paul Pierce who were both great offensive players. They won the NBA Championship in 2007-2008. Probably the best example of a player forgoing his personal stats for the greater good of the team is Chris Bosh. As a Toronto Raptor Bosh averaged 22.8 points per game, but on the championship teams of the Miami Heat, playing with two other superstars, LeBron James and Dwyane Wade, his average dropped to 17.3 points a game. I think everyone who knows basketball and follows the NBA would agree that all three of these players were an equal and vital part of the team's success. These three great players sacrificed their stats to play a role for their teams to win a NBA Championship.

I have tried to be open-minded and fair when using statistics in analyzing the careers of these great players. I do not want to use statistics to make my point, but I want to use the numbers to support my Top 75 in a fair and legitimate way. Statistics obviously play a key role and must be used in selecting the G.O.A.T. but always in the proper context.

6-AWARDS and HONORS

The era in which a player played is very significant. I have seen a lot of changes in the court, 3-point shot, officiating, etc. in my 70+ years watching the NBA. None of these changes have been more impactful than the number of teams in the league and the integration in 1950 of the first black player, Earl Lloyd. When I first started watching on my black and white, 20-inch television in the 50s there were only eight teams. Interestingly, there was only one game televised each week. I know the young fans reading this will have a hard time believing this but every player in the NBA had to get another job because just being a professional basketball player did not pay enough to support a family. The best basketball players in this country competed for the ninety-six positions. It was an honor to play in the NBA and an even greater honor to be recognized with special awards like the Most Valuable Player Award. However, in the early years there might only be 5 players good enough to be considered for that honor; now with 30 teams there might be 20 players that are worthy of such a prestigious award. The MVP award is supposed to recognize the best player of any given year but many times the people who vote have let prejudices and stats determine their pick. Some voters believe that a recipient of the MVP award MUST be on the league's best team. Consequently, the "best" player in the league did not always win the award. The award was not even given before the 1956-57 season so a great player like Dolph Schayes, who was a twelve-time All-star and is considered one of the greatest to ever play never won the MVP Award. His Syracuse team won one NBA championship, but Schayes career which began in 1948-49 was winding down when the award was first presented. The era prior to the introduction of the shot clock in 1954 was naturally an era of considerably fewer points being scored. Schayes, who averaged 18.5 points per game, would be comparable to 25 or more points a game today. Schayes undoubtedly would have won league MVP had the award been given out during the early years of the NBA. MVP awards are significant but like statistics they must be kept in context.

Another very important consideration in choosing the Top 75 is the number of NBA All-Star selections by a player. In the 50s and 60s there were only eight or nine teams so there were only 40 or 45 players to select from (starters plus one) as opposed to today's 30 teams (150 players plus one) the selection to the All-Star team would have been easier and less competitive in the early years. At one time the All-Star team was selected by position: three frontline players and two guards. The number of players that could be chosen from the same team was three until recently when it was changed to four. So, in the era of the great and dominating Boston Celtics team a player like Sam Jones, a true All-Star, might not make the team because the Celtics had a team loaded with all-stars like Bill Russell, Bob Cousy, Tom Heinsohn, and Bill Sharman. Just as the case with the other awards the number of all-star teams a player made must be considered within the context of the era in which he played.

The era also played a role in the number of games and in the level of competition to win a championship. In the earlier years of the NBA a team only had to win one playoff round to make it to the championship round. After the expansion years that began in 1966 the playoffs took on the grueling challenge that it is today. Many NBA basketball gurus base their entire argument for the greatest players of all time on the number of championship teams that they played on. We have all heard the argument "but how many championships did HE win"? I would be the first to concede that it is difficult to have a championship team without great players. I would submit to you that it is a team game, and it takes more than just one player to win a title. A better question might be "is that team great because of that one individual or is the team great because there are several great players on that team"? I have a picture in my office, my favorite, of Jerry West driving to the basket and

Bill Russell trying to block his shot. But what makes the picture so great is that in the background the other players on the court are, John Havlicek, Wilt Chamberlain, Elgin Baylor, and Sam Jones. That one picture has six of the greatest players to ever play in the NBA. All truly great but are they considered the greatest because they played with other great players or are the teams great because of them? Which brings up another question "Is it harder to be great on a great team or be great on a poor team?" A good argument can be made either way. Players that played and won championships are often given too much credit. Several of my Top 75 players never won an NBA title. I don't think that should distract from their overall individual accomplishments and their career. The classic debate for me is the comparison between Russell and Chamberlain. Russell (and the Celtics) won 11 championships while Chamberlain's teams only won two titles. So, does that mean that Russell was the better player? No, not in my opinion. It means that Russell had a better supporting cast, much better in fact. Russell played his entire career with some of the best to ever play in the NBA. The Celtics were also winning all those championships in the era in the NBA when there were only eight teams. So, to say Russell is the best to ever play in the NBA because HE won 11 championships is truly misguided. Statistically, and in the all-important eye test, Chamberlain was a more dominating player than Russell. Russell won 5 MVPs and Chamberlain won 4 but I think even this is misleading. Again, many in the sports media that voted on the award thought that the league MVP should go to the player on the best team. I believe it is an individual award and should go to the best player in the league regardless of the team record or whether the TEAM won the championship or not. I understand the MVP winner should not come from a team that is below .500 or a team that is last in the standings. But just because the MVP was on the championship team does that mean that they won the championship because of him? Maybe so, but maybe he played on a team of other great players like the Celtics in the 60s.

I place greater significance on the awards given to the modern-day recipients than to the players in the earlier years due to the competition for those awards. There are 30 teams in the NBA now, that means there are 150 starters compared to early years where there were 40 starters. As I discussed earlier, it is more difficult now to make the all-star team or be voted the MVP than in the 50s or 60s. Also, many awards such as the All-Defensive Team awards were not presented until the 1968-69 season. The Defensive Player of the Year was first awarded in 1983. So, to say that a player made X number of All-Defensive teams or was voted the best defensive player in the league when the earlier players in the league did not even have an opportunity to compete for the award is mis-leading. Some players have been shortchanged because of the league stipulations pertaining to an award. For example, a player as great as Nate Thurmond never made the All-NBA First Team because the voting was done by position rather than voting for the best player regardless of position. Thurmond was competing against Chamberlain and Russell for the center spot each year. The same could be said about Patrick Ewing. He made one First Team All-NBA but finished in the top 10 in voting 6 times. I don't believe it is fair and equitable to make picks of the best of all time if the picks must be by position. In today's game this is not an issue because most of the great players in the league do not play a specific, defined position. Many of the young great players today play several positions.

I have already discussed the MVP Award and I believe this award, more than any other, plays a significant role in choosing the all-time greatest players and ultimately naming the G.O.A.T. The award, first given in 1955-56 to Bob Pettit, represents the individual player that was chosen the best player for that season. Kareem Abdul-Jabbar won the award the most, six times. Michael Jordan and Russell won the award five times followed by four by Wilt Chamberlain and LeBron James. Larry Bird won the award three consecutive seasons, 1984-1986. Magic Johnson also has won the award three times as has Moses Malone. Twenty-three times the MVP Award has gone to the player whose team won the NBA Championship. Interestingly only two guards won the award prior to Magic in 1986-87, Bob Cousy and Oscar Robertson. Since 1987 there have been 17 guards or half of all the players that received the award were guards. An indication of how the game has changed, and the impact that perimeter players have had on the game. Is it possible to be on this very select and special list of MVP winners and not be considered a Top 75 player of all time? Yes, for example, a player could have been voted in based on the success of his team. In the 65 years since the MVP Award was first presented there has only been a few players that received the award that would not merit a Top 75 pick. The award carries a lot of weight in the selection, but several players are deserving of the Top 75 all-time team but were never an MVP recipient.

My point in discussing the awards was not to diminish the achievement in any way but to emphasize that these honors take on a different significance when comparing different eras. The honors that a player receives each year is an indication of how that person performed in any one given year. I have listed the awards of each player in my Top 75 in their bios because they are significant, but I would caution anyone from putting too much importance on these accomplishments and honors alone.

7-WINNING

Another important criterion in my quest to recognize the best is winning. Too often a player's greatness is based on winning or championships. That is too easy. Winning matters, it is the ultimate goal that is why we keep score! But while I respect Vince Lombardi and consider him one of the top five coaches to ever have coached, in any sport, I do not believe that "winning is the only thing". Neither do I believe that the success of a team is EVER due to the skill or ability of just one player. Tom Brady may well be the best football player to ever play in the NFL, but it is not because HE won 7 Super Bowls. On every one of those teams, he had an outstanding offensive line that gave him time to throw the ball. He had great receivers who got open and caught his passes. A running back or two that kept the defense honest. He played on TEAMS with a defense that made it possible for the team to win without him having to throw 5+ touchdowns a game. It is a team game just as basketball is a team game and every player has a role to play and how well they fulfill their roles has a direct relationship to how successful the team is.

The best teams I ever coached, and the one's that I enjoyed coaching the most, were the teams that had players who were not only talented but unselfish and accepted their role on the team. Why do some teams that have superior talent lose to teams that might have just average players? Simply stated five working together is always better that five working independently of each other. It is referred to as "chemistry" in sports. My coaching hero, John Wooden, had many great slogans that I used and posted in my locker room. One of my favorites was; "It is amazing how much can be accomplished when no one cares who gets the credit." It is very hard to win, losing is much easier. I believe a person can get accustomed to either outcome. Winning requires the sacrifices, determination and commitment from everyone on the team and the bench. I never thought that our high school basketball team was winning just because I was on it. We had players that got rebounds, set screens, contributed to the offense, and played defense. In a much, much bigger arena and a much larger scale the great players in the NBA are winning championships because they are surrounded by players doing the same thing, playing out their role at a very high level. I think that in our society today and in sports particularly, most people like to give too much credit for winning to one person and conversely too much blame to one person for losing. It is much simpler that way, less complicated. Championship teams are made up of more than just one great player, but sports fans like to focus on the ONE who scores the most points. Today it might even mean the one that is considered the best is the one who has the biggest following on the internet or is the most popular. We are always looking for that one special hero to idolize. I think that that is the biggest reason for all the talk and the infatuation over finding and naming a G.O.A.T.

Many fans, perhaps over 50 percent of all NBA fans, have already chosen Michael Jordan as the greatest of all time. He may be but before we crown him, I would like to drill down a little bit and put my criteria to the test. If you ask those fans why they picked Jordan, they will probably say that the number one reason was that HE won 6 NBA Championships. On the surface that sounds like a very convincing argument, a choice based on winning. Some might say that he was a clutch player, he was at his best when the game was on the line. Both are credible, good arguments for making Jordan the G.O.A.T. However, Jordan only made two winning baskets in the playoffs. We seem to remember those more clearly than the one's he missed. We like our heroes. I read where MJ said he has missed more winning shots than he has made but he still wanted the ball in his hands when the game was on the line. That is understandable, a great player is at his best in pressure situations. The great one's always believed they can win the game. As for the six championships Jordan won, his Chicago Bulls team's won 108 and lost 138 in his first three years. (Jordan suffered a broken foot and missed 64 games in that second year.)

After adding Charles Oakley in year two and Horace Grant and Scottie Pippen in year four, the Bulls took off. The 1987-88 team went 50-32 before losing to the dominating Piston's team of the 80s in the second round of the playoffs. They would go on to add Bill Cartwright, Craig Hodges, B.J. Armstrong, John Paxson and Hall of Fame coach Phil Jackson. The Bulls won 6 World Championships in a nine-year span. Now here is the question; Did the Bulls win because of Michael Jordan or because they had a great team, and a great coach? To be sure he was a very, very key part of it, but was MJ THE reason they won? Some might say yes. In choosing a G.O.A.T. winning must be one of the criteria but I think we must guard against making it THE determining factor. Not to belabor the point but in 1993-94 when Jordan "retired" to play baseball the Bulls finished the season 55-27 and lost to the Knicks in seven games in the Eastern Conference Semifinals. Scottie Pippen made the All-NBA 1st Team for the first time in his career, that says a lot about his talent. Jordan was always the "alpha dog" on the Bull's teams, but he had a lot of great players around him. I certainly do not mean to single Jordan out or to diminish his phenomenal career. My point is that just because a player plays on a championship team that does not mean they are the sole reason for the team's success. Based on this one criterion of winning one could make a case for Bill Russell to be crowned the G.O.A.T., after all he is the greatest TEAM winner of all time in any sport!

8-YARDSTICK

The "yardstick" by which every other player is measured speaks volumes to me. I understand when picking the greatest or the best of all time one must take into consideration the era. But greatness has no bounds and knows no limits. Again, I come back to dominance and whether that player was the greatest of his era. There are some individuals that seem to be so superior they become the measuring rod by which all others are judged. Their talents transcend time. A universally accepted best of the best i.e., every new golfer that joins the Professional Golf Tour (PGA) draws comparisons to Tiger Woods. The obvious implication being that Tiger is recognized as the best golfer of this generation. (Many golf fans would disagree and say Jack Nicklaus is the best golfer of this or any generation.) So, is there anyone in the history of the NBA that conjures up that kind of recognition? There are a few examples that come to mind such as in the early days of the NBA every point guard that came into the league was compared to Bob Cousy. Cousy was a tremendous ball handler and passer some would say he was Pete Maravich before there was a "Pistol Pete". In the early days of the NBA power forwards (before they were called power forwards) were compared to Bob Pettit. The big men, who were actually not that big by today's standards, were compared to the first true "BIG" man, George Mikan. Mikan was so dominate that they had to change "the key" (lane) because he was un-guardable that close to the basket. Elgin Baylor was a yardstick of sorts. He was the first player that I saw who could "hang" in the air until the defender came down and then shoot the ball. I heard for years NBA pundits say that no one could hang in the air and do the things that Elgin Baylor could do with a basketball. Great players like Julius Erving, Billy Cunningham, George Gervin, James Worthy, and even Michael Jordan have emulated some of Baylor's moves. The yardstick that has been used since the 80s is Michael Jordan. Many players are still being compared to him i.e., Kobe Bryant, Dwyane Wade, and even LeBron James.

9-CLUTCH

A category that cannot be overlooked in the search for the greatest of all time are the players who perform at their best under pressure_ a CLUTCH player. Who comes to mind when you think of the players that seem to respond best when the situation is most dire or critical? If I listed them all here, I would give away my Top 75 but here are just a few that most fans would recognize: Walt Frazier, Jerry West, John Havlicek, Michael Jordan, Kobe Bryant, Isiah Thomas, Larry Bird, Sam Jones, Magic Johnson, LeBron James, and Rick Barry. The playoffs and the most pressure packed games must be considered when anyone is trying to determine the greatest players of all time for a several reasons; you are competing against the best, there is a lot at stake, the margin for error is much more impactful, there are millions watching, etc. All the players on this list thrive under pressure and live for the special moments of the playoffs. Not everyone on the list would be considered clutch because even on such a unique list as the greatest of all time there are some players that rise above the others. As a coach I was always aware, and I always made my players aware of the player on the other team that we were not going to "let" beat us if we had to double or triple team him. I have made the players performance in the playoffs and in pressure situations an important factor in determining the best.

10-PLAYING BOTH ENDS OF THE COURT

Finally, I think that any player who is worthy of the Top 75 of all-time would have to be considered outstanding on both ends of the court. I don't think that any fan would say that an individual belonged in this elite company just because "they could really shoot the ball". Neither should a player make the team that could not play defense. In an interview with Isiah Thomas, I heard him make this very point about players who may be skilled on offense but not on defense and that "the truly great players play both ends of the court." One of the many common denominators of players in this Top 75 list is that most of the players that led their team and the league in scoring were also great defensive players, rebounders and/or playmakers. They were multi-dimensional, many faceted, and could beat you in many ways! Twenty players that scored over 20,000 points in their career made the All-Defensive Team at least once. The MVP Award is given out each year to that one player that is considered or voted the best player in the league, not just the best offensive player, best defensive player or best rebounder but the best all-around player. In my Top 75, thirty have won the MVP Award. Fifty-two have played on an NBA/ABA Championship team.

Before I get to my Top 75, I have referred to my list as the All-Time NBA Top 75 as well as the best or Top 75 of all time. While the list is dominated by the NBA, I do not believe it is possible to identify the best basketball players of all time and ultimately name the G.O.A.T. and exclude some of the players who began their careers in the American Basketball Association (ABA). The goal here is to recognize the best of the best. I believe that a player like Artis Gilmore should not be slighted simply because he spent the first five years of his professional career in the ABA with the Kentucky Colonels. Gilmore was the ROY (Rookie of the Year) and the MVP in the league in the same year. He also made the All-Time ABA Team. Julius Erving was the best player to ever play in the ABA. He played in the league five years and was the MVP three times and finished second one other year. Dr. J was one of the greatest to ever play in the ABA, NBA or anywhere else. There are several other players from the ABA that are included in my Top 75 based on my criterion.

Perhaps the hardest thing for me to do in picking my Top 75 was to not be biased toward the "older guys", the players I grew up idolizing. As they say the "fish gets bigger the longer you tell the story". I think it is important to keep in mind that over 80 per cent of the NBA players that have ever played in the league have played since the 70s. I have chosen my Top 75 all-time greats using the following era guidelines: the fewest players on the list are from the beginning years to the 60s, a greater percent of the players were chosen from the 60s to the 70s, and the largest percent from the 80s to the present. I don't believe it would be equitable for one-fourth of my Top 75 to be chosen from the early era of the NBA. Based on the expansion of the NBA, the Top 75 must be proportional. Several great "young" players that are in the NBA have a very promising future and one day will be on a best-of-the-best list, they need more time to "prove" they belong. It's called longevity. I have a few pages devoted to these young players under the heading "Top Guns".

As you go thru my list keep in mind that the goal here is to identify the best of the best, NOT the most popular. I have tried to avoid the opinions of the so-called sports authorities or those who have a million followers on their social media platform. I have also purposely avoided studying other's list. I believe that several lists are just copied from someone else's list and little or no criteria is given to justify the picks. You are welcome to criticize just look at my criteria before you get too upset and throw my book in the trash. To summarize and remind you to keep my criteria in mind as you go through the Top 75.

Here again are my guidelines:
1) Dominance
2) Longevity
3) Physicality
4) Winning
5) Statistics
6) Awards
7) Offense vs. Defense
8) Playing both ends of the court
9) Yardstick Test
10) Clutch.

So, without any further ado let's get to THE LIST and a bio of each player.

PLAYER BIOS LEDGER

Career Summary: Pts (Points), Avg (Averages), TRB (Total Rebounds), FG% (Field Goal Percentage), FG3% (3 Point Field Goal Percentage), FT% (Free Throw Percentage)

Recognitions: Blk (Blocked Shots), ROY (Rookie of the Year), STL (Steals), Ast (Assist), POY (Player of Year)

A "gem" could be defined as a unique thing of value, rare, and highly prized. I've included a "GEM" of information for each player.

THE QUEST
TO FIND THE BEST

THE TOP 75
BASKETBALL
PLAYERS OF
ALL TIME

2022 EDITION

BY JACK SUTTER

THE TOP 75 PLAYERS

GRANT HILL

Small Forward/Shooting Guard | 6'8" | 1994-2013

Games	Pts (Avg)	TRB	Assist	FG%	FG3%	FT%
1026	16.7	6.0	4.1	.483	.314	.769

7xAll Star, 5xAll-NBA, ROY, Hall of Fame

Grant Hill would be ranked within the top 50 greatest players if his career had not been cut short by injuries. He was drafted in 1994 by the Detroit Pistons after a great career at Duke. In his first six years in the NBA, he averaged 21.6 points, 7.9 rebounds, and 6.3 assists. He made the All-Star team five of those six years and was in the top 10 in the MVP voting five times. He was considered one of the best all-around players in the league from 1994 to 2000. In 1999, Hill led his team in points, rebounds, and assists for the third time. He led the league in triple doubles 3 straight years, 1996-1998. He began to have ankle injuries in 2000 after being traded to the Orlando Magic, but still averaged 16.4 points over the six years that he played with the Magic. Unfortunately, in his 18-year NBA career Hill was only healthy enough to play in 70 games or more 10 years. He ended his career with 17,137 points, 4,993 rebounds, and 4,252 assists.

❖ After Hill's first 6 seasons in the league, he had 9,393 points, 3,417 rebounds, and 2,720 assists. The only players in the history of the NBA to have better stats in their first 6 seasons were Oscar Robertson, Larry Bird, and LeBron James.

TONY PARKER

Point Guard | 6'2" | 2001-2019

Games	Pts (Avg)	TRB	Assist	FG%	FG3%	FT%
1254	15.5	2.7	5.6	.491	.324	.751

6xAll Star, 4xAll-NBA, 4x NBA Champion, All-Rookie Team, 1x Finals MVP

In one sense or the other every player on this list of Top 75 is a winner but Tony Parker takes it a step further. His Spurs teams won over 1,000 regular season and playoff games. He has played in an unbelievable five NBA Finals and won four of them. He has the most career wins in the playoffs of any point guard in NBA history with 137. (Magic is 2nd with 127 wins.) He scored over 4,000 points in 17 seasons of playoff games (17.9) average and averaged 5.1 assists. He finished his 19-year career with 19,473 points and 7,036 assists (currently 19th all-time). He is one of four point guards to lead a championship team in both scoring and assists for the regular season and the playoffs. (Steph Curry, Isiah Thomas and Walt Frazier are the others.)

❖ Parker's Spurs team won 4 NBA titles and had a 137-89 playoff record. Parker was voted Finals MVP in 2007.

PETE MARAVICH

Point Guard/Shooting Guard | 6'5" | 1971-1980

Games	Pts (Avg)	TRB	Assist	FG%	FG3%	FT%
658	24.2	4.2	5.4	.441	NA	.820

5xAll Star, 4xAll-NBA, All Rookie Team, 1xScoring Champion, 75th Anniversary NBA Team, Hall of Fame.

Pistol Pete had one of the shortest NBA careers of any player on this list. But just like Sandy Koufax in baseball a career cannot always be defined solely by longevity. For several years Maravich was one of the great talents in the NBA. He was among the top five scorers in the league four times. He led the league in scoring in 1976-77 with a 31.1 average. Maravich is 1 of only 10 players in NBA history to average 24 points or more and 5 assists a game for his career. Also, during that 1976-77 season, he led the league in field goal attempts and free throws made. He finished third in the MVP voting that year. Maravich was much more than just a scorer he was a great passer and was like a magician with the basketball. Dan Patrick said this about Pistol Pete on his sports talk show "the ball just looked natural in Pete's hand". Many of the ball handling and dribbling skills that are a part of the game today originated with "Pistol Pete". (The nickname for Pete Maravich may have originally come from a real-life figure from the American Wild West. Frank "Pistol Pete" Eaton who earned his fame from hunting down his father's killers and became a US Deputy Marshall.) Stats alone do not tell the story of the greatness and the career of Pete Maravich. Everyone who saw him play remembers when it was and where they were. Sports fans would stop what they were doing to watch Mark McGwire bat during the 1998 baseball season and basketball fans would stop to watch Pistol Pete play basketball, too. Not everyone on this list is an icon. Maravich is.

⬥ No other player in the history of basketball has had a greater impact on dribbling and ball handling skills than Maravich. His drills are still being taught in basketball camps and to young players today.

DAMIAN LILLARD

Point Guard | 6'2" | 2012-Present

Games	Pts (Avg)	TRB	Assist	FG%	FG3%	FT%
711	24.6	4.2	6.6	.437	.373	.893

6xAll Star, 6xAll-NBA, ROY, 75th Anniversary All-NBA Team

Damian Lillard has more than just one "leg up" on being one of the best players to ever play in the NBA, he has both legs and both feet up. Lillard is one of 3 rookies in NBA history to have 1,500 points and 500 assists in his rookie season. (Oscar Robertson and Allen Iverson also did that.) A complete and dominant player that scores at an elite level. He joined Wilt Chamberlain as the only two players to have 3 or more 60-point games in a season. He also scored over 50 points in multiple playoff games. His team has been in the playoffs in eight of the ten years he has played in the NBA. He has averaged 24.6 points and 6.6 assists in his 10-year career in the regular season and 25.7 points and 6.2 assists in the 8 years he has made the playoffs. He has finished in the Top 8 in the MVP voting 5 times.

◆ Lillard has made two game winning shots to win a playoff series. (Michael Jordan also has two.) He has scored over 60 points in a game three times.

RAY ALLEN

Shooting Guard | 6'5" | 1996-2014

Games	Pts (Avg)	TRB	Assist	FG%	FG3%	FT%
1300	18.9	4.1	3.4	.452	.400	.894

10xAll Star, 2xAll-NBA, All Rookie Team, 2xNBA Champion, 75th Anniversary NBA Team, Hall of Fame

In his rookie season Allen averaged 19.5 points and was among the leaders in made threes as well as free throw percentage. In 2007 he joined the Boston Celtics where he teamed-up with Kevin Garnett and Paul Pierce to make up the "Big Three". The Celtics won the NBA championship in 2008. During this playoff run Allen set records for the most threes scored in the finals and became the first player to make at least seven three pointers in two games in the finals. Allen finished his 18-year career winning one more championship with the Miami Heat in 2013. Along the way he broke Reggie Miller's career 3-point record in playoff games making an unbelievable 385 threes. He finished his career with 2,973 threes, currently second on the all-time list. Allen is currently 6th over-all in free throw pct with .894. He scored 24,505 points. (Currently the 25th most points of all-time.) Only Reggie Miller, Kobe Bryant, and Michael Jordan, as shooting guards, have scored more points in their career. He had 8 seasons over 20 points a game. He played on teams that won 855 games (24th currently all-time) and 100 playoff games. (Currently 25th all-time.)

❖ Only four shooting guards have made more All-Star teams than Allen. (Kobe, Jordan, Dwyane Wade, and Allen Iverson have more All-Star appearances.) Allen is one of three guards in NBA history to average over 18 points a game while shooting over 40% from the 3-point line. (Stephen Curry and Klay Thompson are the others.)

REGGIE MILLER

Shooting Guard | 6'7" | 1987-2005

Games	Pts (Avg)	TRB	Assist	FG%	FG3%	FT%
1389	18.2	3.0	3.0	.471	.395	.888

5xAll Star, 3xAll-NBA, 75th Anniversary NBA Team, Hall of Fame

Reggie Miller's name always comes up when talking about the best pure shooters to ever play in the NBA. He played for 18 years in the league, all with the Indiana Pacers, and scored 25,279 points (18.2) average. Miller did not make the all-defensive team but ask anyone in the NBA that he guarded, and they will tell you that he was an "ornery," tough player. The Pacers played in playoffs in 15 years during Miller's career and he was the main reason. He averaged 20.2 points per game in the playoffs. He was at his best in the playoffs. In his 18-year career he played on 6 teams that made it to the conference finals. One of his teams made it to the NBA Finals. Reggie averaged 24.3 points in those finals against Shaq and Kobe's Lakers. Some NBA fans might question how I could put Miller in my Top 75 when he might not even be the best basketball player in his family. That would be a fair question, but as a coach I can tell you I would have to game scheme for Reggie. He could take over a game offensively, just ask the Knicks.

❖ Reggie Miller ended his career with the highest Effective Field Goal Percentage of any guard in NBA history with an 18+ average per game, which includes Michael Jordan's .509, James Harden's .525, Ray Allen's .530, Allen Iverson .452, George Gervin .507, and Clyde Drexler .495. (Miller ended with a .544.)

SAM JONES

Shooting Guard | 6'4" | 1957-1969

Games	Pts (Avg)	TRB	Assist	FG%	FG3%	FT%
871	17.7	4.9	2.5	.456	NA	.803

5xAll-Star, 3xAll-NBA, 10xNBA Champion, 75th Anniversary All-NBA Team, Hall of Fame

Sam Jones did not get into the NBA until he was 24 years old after serving two years in the Army. Jones was known as "Mr. Clutch" before all the other "Mr. Clutches" came along. He earned the nickname, in part, for his ability to elevate his game in the playoffs. Jones hit a 15-foot jump shot with 2 seconds left in the final game of the Eastern Division finals in 1962 to beat the Warriors. In the 1969 NBA Finals he hit a 17-foot jumper to give the Celtics an 89-88 victory over the Lakers. He averaged almost 19 points a game in the 10 years of play-offs his Celtic team played in. In Jones's 12-year career he never missed the play-offs and only failed to win the NBA Championship twice. The great Celtic teams of this era won 11 championships and Jones led them in scoring in the playoffs three times. Jones played on 10 of those 11 Celtic teams that won the NBA title. He also led the Celtics 5 times in scoring during the regular season. He was the first "small" player I ever saw use the backboard to bank shots in the basket from out on the court.

❖ Sam Jones winning percentage is .718 which is eight all-time among all players in NBA history that have retired.

ADRIAN DANTLEY

Small Forward | 6'5" |1976-1991

Games	Pts (Avg)	TRB	Assist	FG%	FG3%	FT%
955	24.3	5.7	3.0	.540	.171	.818

6xAll Star, 2xAll-NBA, 2xScoring Champion, ROY, Hall of Fame

A drian Dantley was drafted in 1976 by the Buffalo Braves. His first year in the league he averaged 20.3 points and 7.6 rebounds. He is one of 14 players in NBA history to average over 20 points and shoot over 50% in his rookie season. He spent time with five different NBA teams, but his best years were with the Utah Jazz from 1979-1986. During those 7 years he averaged 29.6 points and 6.2 rebounds. In 1981 and 1984 Dantley led the NBA in scoring, averaging just over 30 points each year. Dantley had 4 seasons where he averaged over 30 points a game. (Only Jordan, Wilt and Oscar have more.) In the 1984 and 1985 playoffs he averaged 29 points and 7.5 rebounds. He finished his career with 23,177 points (31st currently on the all-time list) and an outstanding 54.0 percent average from the field. Dantley was one of the most dominating players in the NBA during the 80s.

❖ Dantley is the only player in the history of the NBA to average 24 points a game, have a field goal percentage of 54%, and a free throw percentage of over 80%.

ALONZO MOURNING

Center/Power Forward | 6'10" | 1992-2008

Games	Pts (Avg)	TRB	Assist	FG%	FG3%	FT%
838	17.1	8.5	1.1	.527	.247	.692

7xAll Star, 2xAll-NBA, All-Rookie Team, 2xAll-Defensive Team, 2xBlk Champion, 2xDefensive POY, Hall of Fame

Alonzo Mourning was the 2nd overall pick in the 1992 draft by the Charlotte Hornets. He is 1 of 3 players to average 20 points, 10 rebounds, and 3 blocks a game in their rookie season in the NBA. (Shaq and David Robinson are the other two.) In his first three years with the Hornets, he averaged 21.3 points, 10.1 rebounds, and 3.2 blocked shots. From 1996 to 2002 before he was diagnosed with a kidney disease he averaged 19.8 points, 9.7 rebounds, and 2.9 blocks. "Zo" led the league in blocks in 1998-99 and 1999-2000. He finished second in the MVP voting in 1999 and 3rd in voting for the Most Valuable Player in 2000. In his ten "healthy" years in the NBA he made the All-Star team seven times. He finished his career with 14,311 points, 7,137 rebounds, and 2,356 blocks (currently 11th all-time). He was on the 2005-06 Miami Heat team that won the NBA title.

❖ In Mourning's first 8 seasons in the NBA, he averaged 21 points, 10 rebounds, 3 blocks, and had a .527 field goal percentage. He won 2 Defensive Player of the Year awards. (Only four players have won it more.)

CHRIS WEBBER

Power Forward/Center | 6'9" | 1993-2008

Games	Pts (Avg)	TRB	Assist	FG%	FG3%	FT%
831	20.7	9.8	4.2	.479	.299	.649

5xAll Star, 5xAll-NBA, 1xTRB Champion, ROY, Hall of Fame

Chris Webber was the number one draft pick in the 1993 draft. He was one of the most recognized and publicized college players to come out of the state of Michigan since Magic Johnson. He was a member of the University of Michigan "Fab 5" that took the college basketball world by storm. They were not only great players on the court but off the court they stole the spotlight and introduced the college basketball world into a whole new culture. They were "loud and proud", they wore long, baggy basketball pants and became "rock stars". Webber averaged 17.5 points and 9.1 rebounds in his rookie season in the NBA and for the next nine years averaged 22.8 points, 10.4 rebounds, and 4.6 assists. He averaged 4 assists a game in 10 different seasons which is currently first all-time among power forwards. (Kevin Garnett and Charles Barkley have 9.) He only played 15 games in 1995-96 and parts of seasons after 2003-04. He put up similar numbers in the 10 playoffs to the regular season. In nine healthy NBA seasons he made five All-Star teams and five all NBA teams. He finished fourth in the MVP voting in 2000-2001 and was in the top 10 four other times. He finished his career with 17,182 points and 8,124 rebounds.

❖ Webber was an elite "all around" player at 6'9". He is 1 of 7 players in NBA history to have a 20 point, 10 rebound, 5 assist, 1 steal, and 1 block shot season.

ALEX ENGLISH

Small Forward | 6'8" | 1977-1991

Games	Pts (Avg)	TRB	Assist	FG%	FG3%	FT%
1193	21.5	5.5	3.6	.507	.217	.832

8xAll Star, 3xAll-NBA, Hall of Fame

Alex English was one of the NBA's most prolific offensive players during the 1980s. English was the first player to score 2000 points or more in eight straight seasons. He won the scoring title in the 1982-83 season (28.4) while playing for the Denver Nuggets. Beginning in 1981-82 English made eight straight All-Star teams. In 10 playoffs he averaged 24.4 points and 5.5 rebounds. The "Silent Assassin" finished his 15-year career with 25,613 points. He is one of 8 players in NBA history to score 25,000 points while shooting over 50% from the field. He and LeBron are the only small forwards to do that.

⬧ English is one of 3 players in NBA history to average over 25 points a game at the age of 35 or older. (LeBron and Karl Malone are the other two.) He led the decade of the 80s in scoring.

DAN ISSEL

Center | 6'9" | 1970-1985

Games	Pts (Avg)	TRB	Assist	FG%	FG3%	FT%
1218	22.6	9.1	2.4	.499	.204	.793

7xAll-Star, 5xAll-ABA, All-Time ABA Team, Hall of Fame

Dan Issel is the second all-time leading scorer in the ABA with 12,823 points. He scored 14,659 with Denver in the NBA for a total of 27,482 career points, 12th currently on the all-time list. His Kentucky Colonels team won the ABA championship in 1975 and won a division title in 1972. Issel was a dominating player in the ABA all five years that he played in the league. Issel is one of four players to lead the league (ABA) in scoring as a rookie with a 29.9 average. (Wilt, Spencer Haywood, and Elvin Hayes were the only other three.) At 28 years of age, when he joined the NBA Denver Nuggets, he continued to score at a 21 point a game clip for the next eight years. Though undersized as a 6'9" center in the NBA he still managed to average over 9 rebounds a game.

❖ When Issel retired in 1985 only three players had scored more points in their career. (Kareem Abdul-Jabbar, Wilt Chamberlain and Julius "Dr. J" Erving)

JERRY LUCAS

Center/Power Forward | 6'8" | 1962-1974

Games	Pts (Avg)	TRB	Assist	FG%	FG3%	FT%
829	17.0	15.6	3.3	.499	NA	.783

7xAll Star, 5xAll-NBA, ROY, 1xNBA Champion, 75th Anniversary NBA Team, Hall of Fame

Jerry Lucas came into the league as the number one pick of the Cincinnati Royals in 1962. He also came into the league with chronic knee problems, which would eventually shorten his career. Despite the knee problem he played 11 years and averaged 17 points and over 15 rebounds a game. Lucas is 1 of 4 players to average 20 points and 20 rebounds per game for a season. His last year in 1973-74 his playing time was so limited that his scoring, rebounding and field goal percentage suffered and brought all his career averages down. Lucas was also recognized as being a great passing big man. As a member of the 1972-73 New York Knicks, Lucas played a key backup role in winning a championship. Even with the knee problems, Lucas finished his career with 12,942 rebounds, 17th currently on the NBA all-time list. He has a 15.6 rebound average, which is currently the 4th all-time best. When I got into college coaching in 1970, Jerry Lucas was one of the five best college players I ever saw play.

❀ Lucas and Wilt are the only players in NBA history to have a 20/20 season while shooting over .500 from the field.

ROBERT PARISH

Center | 7'1" | 1976-1997

Games	Pts (Avg)	TRB	Assist	FG%	FG3%	FT%
1611	14.5	9.1	1.4	.537	.0	.721

9xAll-Star, 2xAll-NBA, 4xNBA Champion, 75th Anniversary All-NBA Team

L ongevity is the first word that comes to mind when describing the NBA career of Robert Parish. Parish played in the NBA for 21 years, 14 with the Boston Celtics. A remarkable feat of consistency and longevity. During his career there were only two years, one with the Warriors and his last year with the Bulls, that he played in fewer than 72 games in the season. He finished his career first in the NBA in career games played (1,611). Parish is one of nine players in NBA history with over 20,000 points and 14,000 rebounds. He is currently 29th on the all-time scoring list with 23,334 points. A solid defensive player Parish provided the inside force to help the Celtics win 3 NBA championships in the 80s.

❀ Parish is 1 of 3 players with over 1,000 career wins. (Jabbar and Tim Duncan are the other two.) He won 4 NBA Championships. Only Russell, Jabbar, and Mikan have more titles as centers.

ANTHONY DAVIS

Center | 6'10" | 2012-Present

Games	Pts (Avg)	TRB	Assist	FG%	FG3%	FT%
601	23.8	10.2	2.3	.515	.309	.794

8xAll Star, 4xAll-NBA, 4xAll-Defensive Team, 1xNBA Champion, All-Rookie Team, 75th Anniversary NBA Team

Anthony Davis came into the NBA as the #1 pick out of Kentucky in 2012 as a "can't miss" future NBA star. As a 19-year-old rookie he averaged 13.5 points and 8.2 rebounds for the New Orleans Hornets (Pelicans). Davis went on to play 6 more years with the Pelicans and average 25.4 points and 10.9 rebounds to go along with an average of 2.5 blocked shots. In the two-playoff series he led the Pelicans both years with over 30 points a game. He requested a trade after the 2018 season and was traded to the Lakers where he teamed up with LeBron to win the NBA Championship in 2020. Since the 2020 season Davis has dealt with a series of injuries that have kept him off the court for most of the season. He is one of only four players in NBA history to have a season with 25 points, 10 rebounds, 2 blocks, and 1.5 steals. (He is the only power forward.) Davis was named First Team All-NBA, and First Team All-Defensive player in the same season. In his 10-year career he has still scored 14,318 points, grabbed 6,129 rebounds and led the league 3 times in blocked shots.

◈ Despite injuries Davis is only 28 years old and has already made 8 All Star teams and 4 All-NBA teams.

BILLY CUNNINGHAM

Small Forward | 6'6" | 1965-1976

Games	Pts (Avg)	TRB	Assist	FG%	FG3%	FT%
770	21.2	10.4	4.3	.452	.263	.730

5xAll Star, 4xAll-NBA, 1xAll-ABA, ABA All Time Team, 1xNBA Champion, 1xABA MVP, 75th Anniversary NBA Team, Hall of Fame

Billy Cunningham was called the Kangaroo Kid because he, like Charles Barkley, was an outstanding rebounder for a small forward. Cunningham led the 76ers to six playoffs with a 19.6-point average and 10 rebounds. Along with Wilt Chamberlain, Hal Greer, and Chet Walker the 1967 Philadelphia team won the NBA championship. In those playoffs Cunningham averaged 15 points and 6.2 rebounds a game. After Chamberlain left the 76ers in 1968, Cunningham averaged 24.8 points and 12.8 rebounds and was selected to the first of three straight All-NBA teams. He is 1 of 3 small forwards in NBA history to average 20 points and 10 rebounds a game. (Elgin Baylor and Larry Bird are the other two.) After contesting, in court, a contract dispute with the Carolina Cougars in 1972 it was determined that Cunningham had to honor the contract and join the ABA team. He played the 1972-73 and 1973-74 season in the ABA and lead them to the playoffs. The Cougars went to the ABA finals and Cunningham averaged 24 points and 12 rebounds a game. He was the ABA MVP in the 1972-73 season. He returned to the 76ers in 1974 but suffered a knee injury that ended his career at the age of 32. Cunningham later coached the 76ers and as a head coach finished with a .698 winning percentage, 12th best among coaches in the history of the NBA.

◈ Only 3 other players in NBA history have averaged 20 points, 10 rebounds and 4 assists per game for their entire career. (Wilt, Baylor, and Bird)

PAUL ARIZIN

Forward/Shooting Guard | 6'4" | 1950-1960

Games	Pts (Avg)	TRB	Assist	FG%	FG3%	FT%
713	22.8	8.6	2.3	.421	NA	.810

10xAll Star, 4xAll-NBA, 2xScoring Champion, ROY,
75th Anniversary NBA Team, Hall of Fame

My first memory of the jump shot was seeing Paul Arizin on my black/white TV when he played for the Philadelphia Warriors in the early 1950s. He was "the guy" when talking about scorers in their early days of the NBA. In his second year in the league, he averaged 25.4 points and 11.3 rebounds. He also shot 44.8 percent from the field and 81.8 percent from the free throw line. After a great year in 1951-52 Arizin joined the marines and served in the military for two years. His Warrior teams missed the playoffs only twice during the 10 years that he played. They won the championship in 1956 with Arizin as the leading scorer with a 27.6 average. Arizin was never voted MVP but finished in the top ten in voting four years. (MVP Award did not exist until 1956 which was toward the end of Arizin's career.) He made the All-Star team every year he was in the NBA.

Arizin led the league in scoring with a 25.4 average with no shot clock. (That would equate to over 30 points a game by today's standards.)

BOB MCADOO

Center/Power Forward | 6'9" | 1972-1986

Games	Pts (Avg)	TRB	Assist	FG%	FG3%	FT%
852	22.1	9.4	2.3	.503	.081	.754

5xAll Star, 2xAll-NBA, ROY, 3xScoring Champion, 1xNBA MVP, 2xNBA Champion, 75th Anniversary NBA Team, Hall of Fame

Bob McAdoo was one of the first players that I ever heard referred to as "instant offense". McAdoo put up some unbelievable offensive numbers in the NBA beginning with his second year in the league when he averaged 30.6 points and lead the league in scoring. He also led the league in scoring in his third and 4th year, averaging over 30 points a game each of those seasons. In his first 8 years in the league, he averaged 26.8 points, 11.8 rebounds, and shot .507 per cent from the field. His average never dropped below 21 points. His 1974-75 Buffalo Braves team lost in seven games in the playoffs to the Washington Bullets, but McAdoo averaged over 37 points per game in that series. McAdoo was one of the first big men to step out on the court, face up and score. He was also an outstanding rebounder finishing his career with 8,048 rebounds to go along with 18,787 points. He ended his 12-year career with an NBA championship in 1982 and 1985 with the Los Angeles Lakers in a backup role. McAdoo won an MVP in 1973-74 and finished second to Jabbar two other years.

❖ McAdoo won three consecutive scoring titles. (Only 7 players have done that.)

TRACY MCGRADY

Small Forward | 6'8" | 1997-2013

Games	Pts (Avg)	TRB	Assist	FG%	FG3%	FT%
938	19.6	5.6	4.4	.435	.338	.746

7xAll Star, 7xAll-NBA, 2xScoring Champion, Hall of Fame

Tracy McGrady was a phenom in high school and went straight into the NBA from Mount Zion Christian Academy. In 1997 he was picked 9th overall in the draft by the Toronto Raptors. In his third year he averaged 15.4 points, 6.3 rebounds, and 3.3 assists per game. He led the league in scoring in years six and seven with a 32.1 and 28.0, respectively. He made the All-Star team seven straight years after being traded to the Orlando Magic in 2000. Beginning with the 2000-01 season and going through the 2004-05 McGrady led the Magic with over 30 points per game average in the playoffs. After four years in Orlando McGrady was traded to the Houston Rockets where he teamed up with Yao Ming to get to the playoffs three straight years. In the first playoff series McGrady averaged over 30 points a game. Kobe said "McGrady could do everything on the basketball court that I could do but he was 6'10. He had no weakness in his game. He is the hardest player I have ever had to guard". McGrady scored 18,381 points (73rd currently all-time) in his 13-year career. McGrady made the All-NBA team 7 times and finished in the top 10 in voting for the MVP award 6 times. *See my comments in the introduction of the book about my high school team playing McGrady when he was a junior in high school at Auburndale, Florida.

❖ During an 8 year stretch from 2000-2008 McGrady made 7 All-Star appearances and was voted to the All-NBA team seven times.

DWIGHT HOWARD

Center/Power Forward | 6'9" | 2004-2022

Games	Pts (Avg)	TRB	Assist	FG%	FG3%	FT%
1225	15.8	11.8	1.4	.587	.206	.566

8xAll Star, 8xAll-NBA, 5xAll-Defensive Team, 3xDef POY,
5xTRB Champion, 1xNBA Champion, All Rookie Team

Dwight Howard was the first pick in the 2004 draft by the Orlando Magic right out of prep school at 19 years of age. In his very first year in the NBA Howard averaged 12 points and 10 rebounds a game. He not only had an impact on the offensive end but was a great defensive player making the All-Defensive NBA team five times and being named the Best Defensive Player of the Year three times. He has led the league five times in rebounding and is currently the active player leader with 14,627 rebounds. Howard's overall 58.7 field goal percentage is among the all-time best. For his career Howard's teams have made the playoffs 12 times with a 63-62 record. Howard is averaging 15.3 points and 11.8 rebounds for his career in the playoffs, which earned him the nickname "The Daily Double". He has finished 7th or better five times in the MVP voting. He made the All-NBA team 8 times. (Only 6 centers in the history of the league have more.) His 19,485 career points currently rank him 59th all-time and 11th among active players.

❖ In the 2009-10 season Howard led the league in blocks, rebounds, and field goal percentage. (He is currently the only player to do that.)

ARTIS GILMORE

Center | 7'2" | 1971-1988

Games	Pts (Avg)	TRB	Assist	FG%	FG3%	FT%
1329	18.8	12.3	2.3	.582	.150	.698

11xAll-Star, 5xAll-ABA, 1xMVP-ABA, 5xAll-Defensive ABA, All-Rookie Team, All-Time ABA Team, Hall of Fame

Artis Gilmore was a giant in every sense of the word. He spent his first five years as a pro in the ABA where he averaged over 22 points and 17 rebounds a game. Just as impressive as those numbers is that Gilmore did not miss a game in those first five years. His first year in the NBA with the Chicago Bulls in the 1976-77 season he averaged 18.6 points and 13 rebounds. His 1975 Kentucky Colonels team won the ABA championship. Gilmore averaged 24 points and 18 rebounds during those playoffs. He averaged playing 45 minutes a game, which earned him recognition throughout the league as the "iron man". He was voted the MVP of the 1975 play-offs. Gilmore finished his ABA career as the all-time rebound leader (17.7per game). He was the all-time NBA leader in field goal percentage with a .599 average when he retired in 1988. In his career he finished with 24,941 points, 28th currently all-time. The "iron man" played 18 years and in only 4 of those years did he play fewer than 70 games in the season.

❖ Artis Gilmore was voted the second-best player in the history of the ABA behind the great Dr. J.

JASON KIDD

Point Guard | 6'4" | 1994-2013

Games	Pts (Avg)	TRB	Assist	FG%	FG3%	FT%
1391	12.6	6.3	8.7	.464	.349	.785

10xAll Star, 6xAll-NBA, 5xAst Champion, ROY, 1xNBA Champion, 9xAll-Defensive Team, 75th Anniversary NBA Team, Hall of Fame

Jason Kidd is currently 2nd on the all-time assists and steals leaderboard. However, what sticks out the most about Jason Kidd's career is his longevity. He played for 19 years and a total of 1391 games. One other great quality about Kidd's game is his consistency whether in the regular season or playoffs. He led the NBA 5 times in assists and recorded over 10 assists a game two other seasons but finished second to Magic Johnson. He led the New Jersey Nets to consecutive NBA Finals in 2002 and 2003. He finished his career third all-time in the NBA with regular season triple-doubles (107). Kidd scored 17,529 points, had 8,725 rebounds (most for a point guard) and 12,091 assists. Kidd made First Team All-NBA 5 times. (Only Bob Cousy, Magic Johnson, Jerry West, and Oscar Robertson have more First Team All-NBA selections as point guards.) He was a great leader as a point guard which has served him well as an NBA coach for the past 9 years.

❖ Kidd led the NBA in triple doubles a record 11 times. His 8,725 rebounds are the most in NBA history by a point guard.

CARMELO ANTHONY

Position: Small Forward | 6'7" | 2003-Present

Games	Pts (Avg)	TRB	Assist	FG%	FG3%	FT%
1244	22.5	6.2	2.7	.447	.355	.814

10xAll Star, 6xAll-NBA, 1xScoring Champion, All-Rookie Team, 75th Anniversary NBA Team

Carmelo Anthony came into the NBA in 2003 as a #3 draft pick and a reputation as a great offensive player. He was one of three players to average over 20 points a game as a 19-year-old NBA player. He is 1 of 6 players in NBA history to average over 20 points a game in his first 14 seasons in the league. (Kevin Durant, LeBron, Shaq, Jordan and Jabbar are the others.) Anthony who is playing for his 6th NBA team is still putting up double figure scoring numbers. He has played in 13 playoffs with 4 different teams, but his teams have never made it to the finals even though he has a 23.1-point average in those games. He has played on three Olympic Gold Medal teams. Only 33 players have played in more All-Star games than Anthony. He holds the NY Knicks single game points record with 62.

❖ Anthony's 28,289 career points are currently 9th on the all-time list.

DOMINIQUE WILKINS

Small Forward | 6'8" | 1982-1999

Games	Pts (Avg)	TRB	Assist	FG%	FG3%	FT%
1074	24.8	6.7	2.5	.461	.319	.811

9xAll Star, 7xAll-NBA, 1xScoring Champion, All-Rookie Team, 75th Anniversary NBA Team, Hall of Fame

To say that Dominique Wilkins could soar like an eagle on the basketball court would be an understatement. He was rightly called the "Human Highlight Film". Wilkins could do much more than just jump he was also an offensive human highlight film. He was among the league leaders every year in scoring. In 1985-86 he led the league with a 30.3 points per game average. Wilkins is 1 of 10 players in the history of the NBA to average over 25 points a game for 10 or more seasons. He played twelve of his 16-year career in Atlanta with the Hawks. The Hawks were in the playoffs 8 of those 12 years. In the 10 years that Wilkins made the playoffs he averaged 25.4 points a game. Wilkins is currently 14th in career points with 26,668. The major criticism of Wilkins career was that his team never won a title but that certainly was not a reflection on him as a player. His 1988 Atlanta team took the Celtics to a Game 7 in the Eastern Conference Semifinals before losing to Bird and company. He led the Hawks in scoring during the playoffs and had a playoff high of 47 points against the Celtics in game seven. Wilkins made 9 All-Star teams and 7 All-NBA teams. (Top 50 for both.)

❖ After retiring from the NBA in 1999 Wilkins played in the Euro league for 3 years and won a championship and an MVP Award.

ALLEN IVERSON

Shooting Guard | 6'0" | 1996-2010

Games	Pts (Avg)	TRB	Assist	FG%	FG3%	FT%
914	26.7	3.7	6.2	.425	.313	.780

11xAll Star, 7xAll-NBA, ROY, 1xNBA MVP, 4xScoring Champion, 2xStl Champion, 75th Anniversary NBA Team, 3xAll Star MVP, Hall of Fame

Iverson was a dynamic offensive player. He led the league four times in scoring and led the league in field goal attempts in each of those four years. But what some fans might not realize is that Iverson was an "Iron Man" and averaged playing 42 minutes a game. He led the league in the number of minutes played per game in seven of the 14 years he played in the NBA. Iverson was named Rookie of the Year in 1997. The biggest criticism of Iverson's career is that his team's did not consistently go deep in the playoffs. His playoff record was 30-41. (It takes more than one great player to advance in the playoffs.) Iverson averaged almost 30 points a game in the playoffs. He is #2 all time in career playoff scoring average at 29.7. (Jordan has a 33.4 average.) Iverson is 1 of 4 players in NBA history to lead the league in scoring and steals in the same season. He did it twice. He is currently 26th all-time with 24,368 career points. He was a competitor and believed when the game was on the line, he had to have the ball.

❖ Iverson's 26.6 points per game average ranks him 7th currently all-time.

RUSSELL WESTBROOK

Shooting Guard | 6'3" | 2008-Present

Games	Pts (Avg)	TRB	Assist	FG%	FG3%	FT%
1001	22.9	7.4	8.5	.437	.305	.785

9xAll Star, 9xAll-NBA, All-Rookie Team, 1xNBA MVP,
2xAll-Star MVP, 2xScoring Champion, 3xAst Champion,
75th Anniversary NBA Team

Russell Westbrook became one of only two players in NBA history to average a triple double for a season. (Oscar Robertson was the other.) He has accomplished that feat three other years. The Supersonics, who drafted Westbrook, relocated to Oklahoma City and became the Thunder in 2008. In the 2014 playoffs against the San Antonio Spurs Westbrook scored 40 points, had five rebounds, 10 assists and five steals. He joined Michael Jordan as the only player to post those kinds of numbers in a playoff game. Westbrook's playoff numbers are better than in the regular season. He is currently fifth among active players on the career all-time scoring list with 22,917. Among active players he is 3rd on the list of most assists with 8,492. (11th all-time) He has had 5 seasons averaging over 10 rebounds a game. Westbrook has excelled at getting to the basket and using his athleticism to score points. He is the only player in NBA history to have two scoring titles and two assist titles. Only six point guards have more All NBA picks than Westbrook. Since the 2017-2018 season Westbrook has played for three different teams: Houston, Washington and Los Angeles.

❖ Westbrook has averaged 20 points a game or more for 11 seasons which is #1 all-time among point guards.

KEVIN MCHALE

Power Forward | 6'10" | 1980-1993

Games	Pts (Avg)	TRB	Assist	FG%	FG3%	FT%
971	17.9	7.3	1.7	.554	.261	.798

7xAll Star, 1xAll-NBA, 3xNBA Champion, 6xAll-Defensive Team, All-Rookie Team, 75th Anniversary NBA Team, Hall of Fame

The Boston Celtics made Kevin McHale the number three pick in the 1980 NBA draft. He was the 6th man in his first five years with the Celtics and voted the Sixth Man Award twice in the NBA. McHale spent his entire 13-year career with the Celtics helping them get into the playoffs every year he played. His average in points and rebounds during the playoffs were almost identical to his regular season averages. (17.9 points and 7.3 rebounds) He led the league in field goal percentage in 1987 and 1988 (60.4%). McHale was an incredibly efficient scorer. He is the only player to average 25 points a game, shoot over 60%, and average 2 blocks a game. He made 7 All-Star teams, 3 as a reserve. He finished his career with 17,335 points and 7,122 rebounds.

McHale won 3 NBA Championships and played in five. His overall record as a Celtic is 674-297 (.694%).

STEVE NASH

Point Guard | 6'3" | 1996-2014

Games	Pts (Avg)	TRB	Assist	FG%	FG3%	FT%
1217	14.3	3.0	8.5	.490	.428	.904

8xAll Star, 7xAll-NBA, 5xAst Leader, 2xNBA MVP, 75th Anniversary NBA Team, Hall of Fame

Steve Nash is the personification of a true point guard. Nash has led the NBA 5 times in his 18-year career in assists and has still averaged over 14 points a game. He was known as "Mr. Automatic" at the free throw line with a career 90.4 percentage. He led the league twice in free throw percentage with a 92.1 and a 93.8 average. A Canadian drafted in the first round by the Phoenix Suns, Nash played ten years for the Suns in two different stints. When he joined the Suns in 2004-05, they won 33 more games than the year before he got there. He was named NBA MVP in 2005 and 2006. (Magic and Curry are only other point guards to win the award multiple times.) He played for the Dallas Mavericks from 1998 to 2004 and lead them to the playoffs in four of those six years. Nash is currently fourth all time in assists with 10,335 and 90th all-time in scoring with 17,387 points. Nash is 1 of 11 members of the 50/40/90 club and he did it a record four times. (50% field goal percentage, 40% on 3-point field goals, and 90% from the free throw line for the season) Nash and Bird are the only two players in NBA history to make this elite club more than once.

❖ Currently Nash has the highest 3point shooting percentage of all time for a point guard at .4278 (Curry is at .4276)

DOLPH SCHAYES

Center/Power Forward | 6'8" | 1949-1964

Games	Pts (Avg)	TRB	Assist	FG%	FG3%	FT%
996	18.5	12.1	3.1	.380	NA	.849

12xAll Star, 12xAll-NBA, 1xNBA Champion, 75th Anniversary NBA Team, Hall of Fame

Dolph Schayes was one of the first superstars in all of basketball. He was drafted out of NYU as a college All-American and was inducted into the Naismith college Hall of Fame. Schayes was drafted by the New York Knicks and the Tri Cities Blackhawks. The Blackhawks offered him a larger contract (7500 dollars) so he signed with them and then had his rights traded to the Syracuse Nationals in the NBA. Schayes spent his entire 15-year career in Syracuse and later moved with the team when they went to Philadelphia in 1963 and became the 76ers. Schayes at 6'8" was one of the tallest players in the NBA in his era. He was more known for his outside shooting than his inside play. His patented 2 hand set-shot was copied by several other players in the league. He led the league for three years in free throw percentage and finished his career with an 84.9%. His 1955 National's team won the championship. Schayes led the way with 19 points and 12.8 rebounds in the payoffs. He is currently 71st all-time in scoring with 18,438 points and 29th all-time in rebounds with 11,256. A remarkably durable player Schayes led the league four times in games played and two years in minutes played. He was a 12-time All-Star and 12-time All-NBA player.

From the 1957-58 season thru the 1961-62 season Schayes was the all-time leading scorer and rebounder in NBA history.

DAVID COWENS

Center | 6'9" | 1970-1982

Games	Pts (Avg)	TRB	Assist	FG%	FG3%	FT%
766	17.6	13.6	3.8	.460	.071	.783

7xAll Star, 3xAll-NBA, ROY, 2xNBA Champion, 1xNBA MVP, 3xAll-Defensive Team, 75th Anniversary NBA Team, Hall of Fame

David Cowens was an undersized post player but made up for it with outstanding leaping ability, quickness, and tenacity. In the seven years that he made the playoffs Cowens averaged over 14 rebounds a game. One of the most distinct and unique honors in Cowens career was that in 1972-73 he was the league MVP but failed to make the First Team All-NBA team. He finished 2, 3, 4, and 7 in the voting four other years. His Boston Celtic teams won the championship in 1974 and 1976. Cowens is one of only five players in the history of the NBA to lead their team in points, rebounds, assists, blocked shots, and steals in a single season. He finished his career with 10,444 rebounds, which is currently 35th on the all-time list. He was an excellent passer for a big man, averaging almost four assists a game. He finished his 11-year career with 13,516 points.

❖ In game seven of the 1973 NBA Championship, in which the Celtics won, he had 28 points and 14 rebounds against Jabbar and the Milwaukee Bucks.

JAMES WORTHY

Forward | 6'9" | 1982-1994

Games	Pts (Avg)	TRB	Assist	FG%	FG3%	FT%
926	17.6	5.1	3.0	.521	.241	.769

7xAll Star, 2xAll-NBA, 3xNBA Champion, All-Rookie Team, 1xNBA Finals MVP, 75th Anniversary NBA Team, Hall of Fame

James Worthy was the first pick in the draft by the Los Angeles Lakers in 1982 and played his entire 12-year career as a Laker. Worthy was a 6'9" frontline player who could run the floor, handle the ball, shoot outside, and finish over anyone trying to defend him at the basket. He was also able to elevate his game in the playoffs. Only he and Shaq in NBA history averaged over 20 points a game in the playoffs and shot over 54%. (Minimum 50 games.) Worthy was nicknamed "Big Game James" because of his play in pressure situations. In nine playoffs Worthy averaged over 21 points a game, almost four above his season average. In the 1988 NBA Finals he had one of the best game sevens in playoff history. He scored 36 points, had 16 rebounds, and 10 assists as the Lakers beat the Pistons for the title. He was named Finals MVP. He was a great imitation of Baylor and Dr. J with his ability to seemingly "hang" in the air to get his shot off. The Lakers, with Jabbar, Johnson, McAdoo, Byron Scott, and Michael Cooper along with Worthy were almost unbeatable from 1984 to 1988, winning 3 championships. Worthy is currently 27th all-time with 3,022 playoff points. He scored 16,320 points in his career.

♦ Worthy's regular season record was 622-304 (.672). His playoff record was 96-47 (.671) almost identical to the regular season. He played in 6 NBA Finals and won three of them.

PAUL PIERCE

Small Forward/Shooting Guard | 6'7" | 1999-2017

Games	Pts (Avg)	TRB	Assist	FG%	FG3%	FT%
1343	19.7	5.6	3.5	.445	.368	.806

10xAll Star, 4xAll-NBA, All Rookie Team, 1xNBA Champion, NBA Finals MVP, 75th Anniversary NBA Team, Hall of Fame

Paul Pierce came into the NBA in 1999 out of the University of Kansas with a reputation as a scorer and he lived up to that reputation. In his first year he averaged 16.5 points a game with the Boston Celtics. He went on to average 21.8 points a game in the 15 years he played in Boston. Despite the Celtic deep and rich history Pierce is the only Celtic to lead the NBA in total points in a season with 2,144 points. For his career he played in 14 playoffs and averaged 18.7 points. His 2008 Celtics team with Ray Allen and Kevin Garnett won the championship. Pierce averaged 21.8 points in the series and was voted the Finals MVP. He is currently ranked 16th overall in scoring with 26,397 points. Pierce had a reputation as a clutch player. He had 7 game winning "buzzer beaters". Because of his ability to score in clutch situations Shaq nicknamed him "The Truth".

Pierce was very good at every aspect of the game. He is in the NBA top 100 all-time in points (16th), rebounds (88th), assists (79th), steals (21st), 3 pointers (9th), and free throws made (10th).

GARY PAYTON

Point Guard | 6'4" | 1991-2007

Games	Pts (Avg)	TRB	Assist	FG%	FG3%	FT%
1335	16.3	3.9	6.7	.466	.317	.729

9xAll Star, 9xAll-NBA, 9xAll Defensive Team, 1xStls Champion, All Rookie Team, 1xNBA Champion, 75th Anniversary NBA Team, Hall of Fame

Gary Payton is nicknamed "The Glove" for his ability to "lockdown" an offensive player. Payton is recognized as one of the best defensive players to ever play in the NBA. He made the all-defensive team nine times and led the league in 1995-96 with steals (231). During his 17-year career he also managed to score 21,813 points, which is currently 35th on the all-time NBA list. Payton's teams played in the playoffs in 15 of the 17 years he was in the league. The 2005-2006 Miami Heat team that he played on won the championship. During a ten year stretch from 1994 to 2003 Payton averaged 20.8 points, 7.9 assists, 2.0 steals, made 9 All-NBA teams, 9 All-Star teams, 9 First Team All-Defensive teams and finished in the top ten of the MVP voting 8 times. Payton was the ultimate point guard who could score, play defense, run the team and get the ball in the hands of the right guy at the right time. He currently ranks 10th all-time with 8,966 assists, and finished his career with 2,445 steals, which is currently fifth all time. He is currently 13th all-time in career minutes played.

❖ Payton made All-NBA and All-Defensive team in the same season 9 times, a record for point guards.

WILLIS REED

Center | 6'9" | 1964-1974

Games	Pts (Avg)	TRB	Assist	FG%	FG3%	FT%
650	18.7	12.9	1.8	.476	NA	.747

7xAll Star, 5xAll-NBA, 2xNBA Champion, 2xNBA Finals MVP, All Rookie Team, 1xAll-Defensive Team, 75th Anniversary NBA Team, Hall of Fame

Willis Reed played in the NBA for 10 years all with the New York Knicks. He played in seven playoffs and is best known for his gallant effort in the 1973 NBA Finals against the Lakers, which the Knicks won. Reed hobbled on one leg for much of the series. He was not the leading scorer or rebounder in the series but was still chosen the MVP of the series. He played in all 17 games of the playoffs and averaged 12.5 points and 8 rebounds. His 1970 Knicks team also won the NBA championship with Reed averaging 23.7 points and 13.8 rebounds per game in the playoffs. In 1970 he won the league MVP, All-Star MVP, and the Finals MVP becoming the first player in NBA history to win all three awards in the same season. (Jordan and Shaq are the only other players to do this.) Reed finished his 10-year career with 8,414 rebounds (currently 64th all-time) and 12,183 points.

◆ Reed's career was cut short with injuries but in 10 years in the NBA he made 5 All-NBA teams and 7 consecutive All-Star teams.

JOHN STOCKTON

Guard | 6'1" | 1984-2003

Games	Pts (Avg)	TRB	Assist	FG%	FG3%	FT%
1504	13.3	2.7	10.5	.515	.384	.826

10xAll Star, 11xAll-NBA, 5xAll-Defensive Team, 2xStl Champion, 9xAst Champion, 75th Anniversary NBA Team, Hall of Fame

John Stockton's nickname was not "Mr. Assist", but it could have been. Stockton led the NBA in assists nine straight years beginning in 1987-88 season. He played his entire 19-year career with the Utah Jazz and played a major role in them making the playoffs each of those years. Stockton has the most career wins of any point guard in NBA history with 953. (.633-win percentage) He is currently the all-time assist leader with 15,806 assists and has the highest assist average ever in a single season with 14.5 in 1989-90. Stockton also finished as the all-time steals leader with 3,265. (Jason Kidd is 2nd with 2,684.) He played 47,764 minutes. (Currently 10th all-time.) Magic Johnson once called John Stockton the greatest team leader he had ever played against. Stockton is 1 of 26 players to make 10 All-Star teams and 10 or more All-NBA teams. It is fitting that the two statues standing outside the Utah Jazz arena have Stockton and Karl Malone near each other. A ball screen and a bounce pass away!

❖ Stockton was an elite point guard both offensively and defensively, but his greatest asset was his durability. He played every game in 17 of his 19 seasons in the league.

GEORGE GERVIN

Shooting Guard/Small Forward | 6'7" | 1974-1988

Games	Pts (Avg)	TRB	Assist	FG%	FG3%	FT%
1060	25.1	5.3	2.6	.504	.271	.841

12xAll Star, 7xAll-NBA, 2xAll-ABA, ABA All-Time Team,
4xNBA Scoring Champion, All Rookie Team,
75th Anniversary NBA Team, Hall of Fame

George Gervin has one of the "coolest" nicknames in the history of the NBA, "Iceman". He earned that nickname from the way he played, always under control and cool. Some say he earned that nickname because no one ever saw him sweat. In his 14-year career in the ABA and NBA his teams only failed to make the playoffs one time. Gervin's career playoff scoring average was an impressive 26.5 points per game. Gervin, like Doctor J, and MJ, had that knack for defying gravity and floating in the air to get to the basket and score. He is still remembered for his "finger roll". Gervin was a dynamic offensive player who could score outside or with unbelievable drives to the basket, usually finishing with that finger roll. He is the only guard in NBA history to score over 20,000 points with a field goal percentage over .500. He led the NBA in scoring three consecutive years. He made 9 All-NBA/ABA teams. (Only Kobe and Jordan as shooting guards have more.) Gervin finished his career with 26,595 points, currently 17th on the all-time list.

❖ Gervin is one of five players in NBA history to have 4 or more scoring titles. (Wilt had 7 and Jordan had 10)

BOB COUSY

Point Guard | 6'1" | 1950-1963

Games	Pts (Avg)	TRB	Assist	FG%	FG3%	FT%
924	18.4	5.2	7.5	.375	NA	.803

13xAll Star, 12xAll-NBA, 8xAst Champion, 6xNBA Champion, 1xNBA MVP, 75th Anniversary NBA Team, Hall of Fame

There is a reason they called Bob Cousy "Houdini of the Hardwood". He was the first professional basketball player, outside of the Globetrotters, to ever go between his legs and behind his back with the basketball during the game. (And he did it often.) He was a true magician with the basketball. A lot of the reason for the Celtic's success in the 50s is due to the leadership of Cousy. "Cooz" controlled the tempo and got the ball to the right guy at the right time while still managing to average over 18 points a game. He made the All-Star team every year he played in the NBA and only missed making the All-NBA team his first year. (Cousy did play in 7 games in the 1969-70 season and did not make the All-Star team or All NBA team.) He led the league in assists eight of the 13 years he played. (Only Stockton with 9 has more.) He is currently ranked 100th in scoring with 16,960 points and 20th in assists with 6,955. Cousy finished in the top 8 in the MVP voting eight times winning it in 1956-57. He was the first point guard to ever win the league MVP. Bob Cousy set the bar very high for point guards in the NBA.

❖ Cousy and West were voted to the All-NBA team 12 times as point guards, which is the most for a point guard in the history of the NBA.

CHRIS PAUL

Point Guard | 6'0" | 2005-Present

Games	Pts (Avg)	TRB	Assist	FG%	FG3%	FT%
1155	18.1	4.5	9.5	.473	.369	.871

*12xAll Star, 11xAll-NBA, 9xAll-Defensive Team, 6xSTL Leader,
5xAst Champion, ROY, 75th Anniversary NBA Team*

Chris Paul a first-round draft pick by the New Orleans Hornets (Pelicans) is still making ripples if not waves in the NBA in his 17th season. Paul averaged 16.1 points and 7.8 assists a game his first year in 2005-06. He averaged 14.7 points and finished second in assists with 10.8 this past season. In his 17-year NBA career Paul has only missed the playoffs three years. He has led the league in assists five times and led the league in steals six times. Paul has been in the top ten in the MVP voting ten times, finishing second in the voting in 2007-08. He is sixth among active players with 20,936 points and 1st among active players in assists with 10,977. Paul is 4th all-time with 2,453 steals and is likely to pass Gary Payton and Michael Jordan on that list and finish third behind John Stockton and Jason Kidd. He is the only point guard in NBA history with 20,000 points and 10,000 assists. (Only LeBron has done this.) Paul led the league in assists and steals in the same season 3 times. (Only player in NBA history to do that.)

❖ Paul has played in 12 All-Star games. (Only Cousy and West as point guards have been in more.) He is 6th all-time in the NBA by point guards in winning percentage .650 (751-404).

KAWHI LEONARD

Small Forward | 6'7" | 2011-Present

Games	Pts (Avg)	TRB	Assist	FG%	FG3%	FT%
576	19.2	6.4	2.9	.493	.384	.858

5xAll Star, 5xAll-NBA, 2xNBA Champion, All-Rookie Team, 2xFinals MVP, 7xAll-Defensive Team, 1xSTL Champion, 2xDef POY, 75th Anniversary NBA team

Kawhi Leonard is one of the best "all around" basketball players in the NBA. One of the criteria to make the Top 75 in the NBA is to be able to make an impact on both ends of the court, offensively and defensively. Leonard passes the test with flying colors. His teams have been in the playoffs nine years of his 10-year career. Since the 2015 playoffs he has averaged 27.7 points and 8.2 rebounds a contest. His 2014 Spurs team and the 2019 Raptors team won the NBA Championship. In 2019 he averaged 28.5 points and 9.8 rebounds in the finals. Leonard has been named the Finals MVP with TWO different teams. He has finished in the top ten in the voting for the league MVP five times. Leonard is third among active players in steals per game (1.8). He is the only small forward in NBA history to win defensive player of the year two or more times. At 29 years of age Leonard has made 5 All-Star teams, 5 All-NBA teams and 7 All-Defensive teams.

 Leonard currently has the highest winning percentage of all time in NBA history with a minimum of 500 games (429-147) .744% and 86-49 playoffs .637%. Clutch and winner in spades!

CLYDE DREXLER

Shooting Guard | 6'7" | 1983-1998

Games	Pts (Avg)	TRB	Assist	FG%	FG3%	FT%
1086	20.4	6.1	5.6	.472	.318	.788

10xAll Star, 5xAll-NBA, 1xNBA Champion, 75th Anniversary NBA Team, Hall of Fame

Every NBA player has a nickname but not many have a nickname that identifies that player as much as "Clyde the Glide" identifies Clyde Drexler. Drexler could seemingly float through the air for countless seconds to reach his final destination the basket and a score. His style was honed during his glory days in college with the Houston Cougars and continued into the NBA with the Portland Trailblazers. He went back to the Houston Rockets in 1994 where he finished his career. Drexler was a great scorer with an exceptional midrange jumper and the ability to get the ball to the basket. He averaged 20.4 his career and ironically the exact same average in all 15 playoffs he played in. In 1995 the Rockets led by Drexler's 21.5 points per game and Hakeem Olajuwon's 27.8 points beat the Orlando Magic in four straight games to win the NBA championship. Drexler is currently 34th all-time in career points with 22,195 points, and 36th all-time with 6,125 assists. Drexler is 1 of only 2 players in NBA history with 20,000 points, 6,000 rebounds, 6,000 assists, and 2,000 steals. (LeBron is the other player.) Only Jordan and Wade as shooting guards have more blocks.

In a 12 year stretch in his NBA career Drexler averaged 22 points, 6.6 rebounds, 6 assists, 2 steals and 1.8 blocks.

JAMES HARDEN

Shooting Guard | 6'5" | 2009-Present

Games	Pts (Avg)	TRB	Assist	FG%	FG3%	FT%
923	25.0	5.6	6.7	.443	.362	.859

10xAll Star, 7xAll-NBA, 3xScoring Champion, All-Rookie Team, 1xNBA MVP, 75th Anniversary NBA Team

It took James Harden a couple years to learn his way in the NBA but since his 4th year he has never scored less than 21 points a contest. He has led the league three times in scoring with an average over 30 points a game. He also has managed to average 6.8 assists during his 13-year career. He led the league with 11.2 assists a game in the 2016-17 season. Harden has played for 2 different teams after an 8-year stint with the Houston Rockets. He is a great offensive player and shooter especially with his signature step back jumper from "downtown". He is the first player in NBA history to score 2,000 points, get 900 assists, and 600 rebounds in a season. Harden has led the NBA in 3-pointers 3 times. (Only Curry with 7 has more.) He is currently 28th overall in scoring and fourth among active players with 23,477 points. He is also 6th on the active player list for assists and 31st overall with 6,397. He is #1 all-time in 30 point and 10 assists games with 99. (LeBron has 94.) Harden was the MVP in the league in 2017-18 and has been in the top 10 in votes eight times. He made the All-NBA First Team 6 times, only shooting guards with more are Kobe and Jordan. Considered one of the best shooting guards of all time Harden could make it into the top ten NBA scorers before his career is over. He is 1 of 10 players in NBA history to have over 20,000 points, 6,000 assists, and 5,000 rebounds. Harden is the only player to lead the NBA in total points, total assists, and total steals in his career. He averaged 30 points per game in three different seasons. He also averaged 10 assists per game in three different seasons.

Harden has led the league in points, assists, steals, free throws, 3 pointers, and minutes played at some point in his career. (No one else has done that.)

SCOTTIE PIPPEN

Small Forward | 6'8" | 1987-2004

Games	Pts (Avg)	TRB	Assist	FG%	FG3%	FT%
1178	16.1	6.4	5.2	.473	.326	.704

7xAll Star, 7xAll-NBA, 6xNBA Champion, 10xAll-Defensive Team, 1xStl Champion, 75th Anniversary NBA Team, Hall of Fame

Scottie Pippen is one of only 11 basketball players to come out of a NAIA program and make All-NBA. He was an integral part of the Bulls 6 NBA championships. Pippen was much more than Robin (to Jordan's Batman) in the Bulls organization. He is 1 of 5 players in NBA history to lead his team in points, rebounds, steals, assists, and blocks for a season. He has the most All-Defensive selections of any small forward in NBA history (10). Pippen is arguably the best small forward defender of all time. Due to his length and athleticism, he was a great "on ball" defender. He finished in the top 10 in the MVP voting six times. During the Bulls 6 championship playoff runs Pippen had more rebounds, assists, steals, and blocks than Jordan. He is currently 64th in career points with 18,940 points, 90th all-time with 7,494 rebounds, and is currently 35th on the all-time assists list with 6,135. He is also 7th on the NBA all-time list with 2,307 steals.

Everyone knows Pippen played on 6 NBA Championship teams but what NBA fans might not know is he has a better winning percentage than his teammate, Jordan. Pippen's career win-loss record is 810-368 (.687) and MJ's is 706-366 (.659).

WALT FRAZIER

Point Guard | 6'4" | 1967-1980

Games	Pts (Avg)	TRB	Assist	FG%	FG3%	FT%
825	18.9	5.9	6.1	.490	NA	.786

7xAll Star, 6xAll-NBA, 7xAll-Defensive Team, 2xNBA Champion, All-Rookie Team, 75th Anniversary NBA Team, Hall of Fame

I said in the beginning of writing this book that I would not let my personal biases get in the way of my selection of this Top 75 NBA team. But I am human, and I do have my personal favorites. I grew up about 30 miles from Carbondale, IL where Southern Illinois University is located and where I saw Frazier play several times in college. I also became friends with Frazier's college coach Jack Hartman. Coach Hartman helped me get the head coaching job at Butler County CC in Kansas in 1979 when he was winning big eight championships at Kansas State University. Frazier or "Clyde," as he was called, led SIU to an NIT championship in 1967. (Clyde was the nickname Knicks coach Red Holtzman gave him, from the movie Bonnie and Clyde, because of his "cool" demeanor.) He used those leadership qualities to lead the New York Knicks for 10 years, including two NBA championships. Frazier was an exceptional athlete and at 6'4" and 200 lbs. with long arms and deceptive quickness he was the perfect size for a point guard. He could score on midrange jumpers or by taking the ball to the basket. Jerry West has been quoted as saying that Frazier was the toughest guard for him to score on. He made All-NBA First Team and All-Defensive First Team in the same season. He did it 4 times, the most of any point guard. In five of the 8 playoffs that the Knicks were in Frazier was the leading scorer with over 20 points a game. Frazier had an exceptional

49% field goal percentage and an outstanding 5.9 rebounds a game as a point guard. "Clyde" finished his career with 15,581 points, 4,830 rebounds, and 5,040 assists. In the Knicks 1970 NBA Championship Finals game seven win over the Lakers against Wilt, Baylor, and West, Frazier scored 36 points, had 19 assists, and got 7 rebounds. He was the first point guard to lead a championship team in scoring during the regular season and in the playoffs. Frazier in addition to being one of the "smoothest" and "coolest" dudes on the hardwood was just as cool and stylish off the court. He finished his 13-year NBA career in Cleveland, but he was a New York Knickerbocker to the bone.

Frazier is the only point guard in NBA playoff history to average 20 points a game and shoot over 50% from the field for a career.

ISIAH THOMAS

Point Guard | 6'1" | 1981-1994

Games	Pts (Avg)	TRB	Assist	FG%	FG3%	FT%
979	19.2	3.6	9.3	.452	.290	.759

12xAll Star, 5xAll-NBA, 1xAstChampion, 2xNBAChampion, 1xFinals MVP, 75th Anniversary NBA Team, Hall of Fame

The first time I saw Isiah Thomas play I knew he was destined for greatness as a basketball player. I was at the Illinois high school state tournament on the campus of the University of Illinois in 1975 watching this 9th grader from Saint Joseph High School playing like he was a senior, controlling the entire game. I have seen thousands of high school players while scouting and recruiting and Isiah Thomas is one of the best I have ever seen. As everyone who follows college basketball knows Thomas went on to lead Indiana University to a national championship in 1981 before declaring for the NBA draft that same year. Thomas was the 2nd player chosen in the draft by the Detroit Pistons. He played his entire 13-year career with them and led them to back-to-back NBA Championships in 1989 and 1990. He led the Pistons in scoring and assists during the regular season and playoffs for those championship teams. (Only point guard to do that twice.) It is not too difficult to see a theme or pattern here with Isiah Thomas career:1) he is a winner 2) he is a great leader. Isiah was a 12-time NBA All-Star selection, only 14 players have more selections. Inexplicably, despite the Piston's success in the 80s Isiah did not make the All-NBA team in 1989 or 1990. He led the league in assists in 1984-85 and every year he played he averaged eight assists or more. He is 1 of 3-point guards to average 19 points and 9 assists per game for a career. (Oscar and

Magic are the other two.) Just like in the Illinois state high school tournament, where the stakes are high, Thomas always seemed to rise to the occasion. He is currently 67th all-time in points with 18,822, 9th in assists with 9,061, and 17th in steals with 1,861.

In game 6 of the 1988 finals Thomas scored 25 points in the THIRD quarter on one leg. He finished with 43 points, but the Pistons lost by 1 to the Lakers.

RICK BARRY

Small Forward | 6'7" | 1965-1980

Games	Pts (Avg)	TRB	Assist	FG%	FG3%	FT%
1020	24.8	6.7	4.9	.456	.297	.893

12xAll Star, 6xAll-NBA, 1xScoring Champion, 1xNBA Champion, 1xStl Champion, ROY, 4xAll-ABA, 1xFinals MVP, ABA All-Time Team, 75th Anniversary NBA Team, Hall of Fame

Rick Barry began his NBA career as a "scoring machine" and continued to score at a 26.9 per game clip for 12 years in the ABA/NBA. In his first three playoffs, one with the San Francisco Warriors and three in the ABA, he averaged almost 34 points a game. Barry was much more than just a scorer; he led the league in 1974-75 in steals and averaged almost five assists a game for his career. Despite all the offensive numbers he might have been known best for his uncanny ability to make free throws, underhanded. He led the league seven times in free throw percentage. He led the Golden State Warriors to the NBA championship in 1975 with 30.6 points average, 6.2 assists and won the Finals MVP Award. He has the highest scoring average in NBA Finals history with a 36.3 average. Barry finished his career with a total of 25,279 points, which is currently 25th all-time. He holds the record for the best per game points average in ABA history with a 30.5 average. Barry was All-NBA/All-ABA 10 times.

❈ Barry is the only player in basketball history to lead the NCAA, the ABA, and the NBA in scoring.

GIANNIS ANTETOKOUNMPO

Forward/Guard | 6'11" | 2013-Present

Games	Pts (Avg)	TRB	Assist	FG%	FG3%	FT%
656	21.8	9.4	4.6	.535	.288	.718

6xAll Star, 6xAll-NBA, 1xNBA Champion, All-Rookie Team,
5xAll-Defensive Team, 1xDef POY, 2xNBA MVP, 1xFinals MVP,
75th Anniversary NBA Team

I f you look up basketball stats, you probably use Basketball Reference as I do for my information. On the Basketball Reference website, it has Giannis's position listed as; small forward, power forward, point guard, and shooting guard. In other words, he can play anywhere on the court and does. The website also lists his nickname as the "Greek Freak", which says it all. Giannis came into the NBA in 2013 as a 19-year-old. He has averaged 21.8 points in his nine-year career and even a more impressive 26.8 points in the five playoffs he has played in. His 2021 Bucks team won the championship with him leading all scorers in the Finals with 35.2 points a game, 13.2 rebounds and 5.0 assists. He scored 50 points in the series clinching game 6 and won the Finals MVP. In addition to winning two league MVP's, he has finished 3rd, 4th, 6th, and 7th in the voting four other years. Among active players he is 13th in scoring and 14th in rebounding. Giannis is perhaps the most phenomenal player in the NBA today and at 28 years of age and with good health he could end up in the top five all-time greatest basketball players. Maybe even be the future G.O.A.T.

❖ Giannis is the only player in the history of the NBA to average 25 points, 10 rebounds, 5 assists, 1 steal, 1 block in MULTIPLE seasons. Only 4 other players have done it once Giannis has done it 4 times.

DIRK NOWITZKI

Power Forward | 7'0" | 1998-2019

Games	Pts (Avg)	TRB	Assist	FG%	FG3%	FT%
1522	20.7	7.5	2.4	.471	.380	.879

14xAll Star, 12xAll-NBA, 1xNBA Champion, 1xNBA MVP, 1xFinals MVP, 75th Anniversary NBA Team

D irk Nowitzki was drafted over 20 years ago by the Milwaukee Bucks but unfortunately, for them, they traded him to the Dallas Mavericks, where he played his entire 21-year career. Nowitzki, who was born in Germany, and is regarded as one of the greatest power forwards of all time. He is the first European player to ever make the first team All-NBA team, first to play in an All-Star game, and the first to be voted NBA MVP. A great outside shooter Nowitzki was one of the first seven footers to consistently score facing up to the basket, from 30 feet. In 1998 when he entered the league, he was a thin 19-year-old who had entered the NBA right out of prep school. In his first year he was intimidated by the physical play in the league and wasn't sure he could ever play in the NBA. After that first year he found his niche as a power forward shooting jumpers out on the floor. Nowitzki led the Mavs to the NBA championship in 2011 with a 26-point average in the NBA Finals. The Mavericks made the playoffs in 15 of Nowitzki's 21-year career. He finished his career with 31,560 points (currently 6th all time) and 3,663 playoff points (17th all-time). He is currently 26th all-time in rebounding with 11,489 rebounds and 18th all-time in free throw percentage. Nowitzki finished his career as 1 of only 5 players in NBA history to score 30,000 points and get over 10,000 rebounds. (Jabbar, K. Malone, Wilt and LeBron are the others.) He is 1 of

9 members of the 50/40/90 club. Nowitzki was not the first "big man" who could score from 30 feet, but he refined the art and revolutionized how a big man could be an offensive threat from out on the court.

❖ Only 7 players have made more All-Star teams and only 6 players have made the All-NBA team more than Nowitzki.

DWYANE WADE

Shooting Guard | 6'4" | 2003-2019

Games	Pts (Avg)	TRB	Assist	FG%	FG3%	FT%
1054	22.0	4.7	5.4	.480	.293	.765

13xAll Star, 8xAll-NBA, 3xAll-Defensive Team, 1xScoring Champion, 1xNBA Finals MVP, All-Rookie Team, 75th Anniversary NBA Team

Dwyane Wade began his NBA career with the Miami Heat as the 5th overall pick in the 2003 draft. After that first year in the NBA Wade's career took off and for the next 13 years, he was one of the best and most versatile players in the NBA. Wade led the league in scoring in the 2008-09 season and managed to dish out 7.5 assists per game. He led the Heat to the first of their three NBA championships in 2006 with a 27.4 regular season average. In the Finals he averaged 34.7 points and was named the Finals MVP. He was joined during the 2011-12 season by LeBron James and Chris Bosh to form the "Big Three" and win two more NBA titles in 2012 and 2013. Wade, who was known as a great mid-range shooter made over 48% from the field. He finished his 17-year career playing with the Heat after going to the Bulls in 2016 and later played with the Raptors and the Cavs. He played in his last and 13th all-star game as a 37-year-old. (Only 10 players have played in more All-Star games.) He also made 8 All-NBA teams. (Only Kobe and Jordan made more All-NBA teams as shooting guards.) Wade finished his career with 23,165 points, currently 32nd all-time and 5,701 assists, currently 43rd.

❖ Wade is one of only three players in NBA history to score over 20,000 points, 5,000 assists, 4,000 rebounds, 1,500 steals, 800 blocks, and make 500 3 pointers in a career.

JOHN HAVLICEK

Small Forward/Shooting Guard | 6'5" | 1962-1978

Games	Pts (Avg)	TRB	Assist	FG%	FG3%	FT%
1270	20.8	6.3	4.8	.439	NA	.815

13xAll Star, 11xAll-NBA, 8xNBA Champion, All-Rookie Team, 8xAll-Defensive Team, 1xFinals MVP, 75th Anniversary NBA Team, Hall of Fame

The Boston Celtics made John Havlicek their number one draft pick in 1962 and 16 years later he retired as an all-time Celtic great. "Hondo" a nickname inspired by John Wayne in the 1953 movie Hondo. Havlicek earned the nickname honestly by his toughness, his grit, and his seemingly unending movement on the basketball court. In his first seven years he was recognized as the best 6th man in the NBA. He made All-NBA 4 times, as a reserve. In 1970-71 and in 1971-72 he led the league in minutes played. He was considered one of the toughest players in the NBA to guard because of his constant motion. Havlicek is one of only three NBA players with a perfect 8-0 record in the finals. (KC Jones and Satch Sanders are the other two.) He won 8 NBA Championships, and his career playoff series record is an incredible 26-5. Havlicek is perhaps remembered most for his steal against the 76ers in the 1965 Eastern Conference championship game when he tipped an inbounds pass from Hal Greer of the 76ers to teammate Sam Jones to ice the game for the Celtics. Earl Strom, veteran NBA referee, said in his 32 years in the NBA it was one of the greatest plays he ever saw. Hondo is currently ranked 17th all-time with 26,395 points, 74th with 8,007 rebounds, and 37th with 6,114 assists. Like many of the other players on this Top 75 list of greats he had an unbelievable winning percentage at every level he played. Havlicek is currently 14th all-time in minutes played with 46,471. *As I referenced earlier in the book his Ohio State team was one of the best college teams I ever saw.

⬧ Havlicek is one of six players in NBA history with 20,000 points, 6,000 rebounds, and 6,000 assists for a career.

ELGIN BAYLOR

Small Forward | 6'5" | 1958-1972

Games	Pts (Avg)	TRB	Assist	FG%	FG3%	FT%
846	27.4	13.5	4.3	.431	NA	.780

11xAll Star, 10xAll-NBA, ROY, 75th Anniversary NBA Team, Hall of Fame

Elgin Baylor was the first basketball player that I ever saw that made playing basketball look like a ballet. Baylor was the original "hang in the air" player until everyone else came down and then he would score the basketball. He seemed to defy gravity, he was the original Dr. J. Baylor was drafted by the Minneapolis Lakers and played his entire 14-year career as a Laker. In his first year in the league, he averaged 24.9 points and 15.0 rebounds. Baylor averaged almost 33 points a game in his first 6 playoffs in Minneapolis and in Los Angeles. The year before "Elg" joined the Lakers the team won only 19 games, the worst record in the NBA. The franchise was about to go under. He is credited with singlehandedly saving the franchise with his dynamic play and on the court charisma. The first year he was with the Lakers they went 33-39. The Lakers lost in the finals to the Celtics that year. Baylor never won an MVP. The league MVP was usually awarded to the best player on the best team, which was usually the Celtics. He finished second and 3rd three times in the voting for the prestigious award. He is 1 of 11 players to make First Team All-NBA 10 or more times. Jerry West joined the Lakers in the 1961-62 season. They became known as "Mr. Inside and Mr. Outside". The Lakers won the Western Division but lost again to the Celtics 3-4 in the finals. Baylor scored 61 points in an NBA Final and scored 284 points in the series finals.

(The most points ever in a finals series.) Baylor is currently 33rd all-time in scoring with 23,149 points and 27th all-time in rebounds with 11,463. I loved watching Baylor on the basketball court with the ball in his hand and that "head bob".

❖ Baylor is one of only four players in NBA history to average 20 points, 10 rebounds, and 4 assists for a career.

BOB PETTIT

Power Forward/Center | 6'9" | 1956-1967

Games	Pts (Avg)	TRB	Assist	FG%	FG3%	FT%
792	26.4	16.2	3.0	.436	NA	.761

11xAll Star, 11xAll-NBA, 2xScoring Champion, 1xNBA Champion, ROY, 2xNBA MVP, 75th Anniversary NBA Team, Hall of Fame

I grew up about 100 miles from St. Louis and as a 10–11-year-old kid in the 50s when I was playing basketball on my outside dirt court, I was always Bob Pettit. He came into the NBA out of LSU with a great jump shot, a one-handed free throw shot, and an unbelievable competitive work ethic. Pettit was the first recipient of the NBA MVP award in 1956. He won the award again in 1959 and could have won it four straight years but the award was going to players on the Boston Celtics who were winning championships. (Cousy and Russell) In nine of his eleven years in the NBA Pettit finished in the top six in MVP voting. Pettit led the league in scoring twice. Ironically, in the year, he averaged over 31 points, he lost the scoring championship to Wilt Chamberlain who averaged an unbelievable 50.4 points per game. He is currently 41st all-time in scoring with 20,880 points (8th in average) and 18th all-time in rebounds with 12,849. Pettit was a great free throw shooter finishing 21st all-time in free throws attempted and made. The decade of the 50s in the NBA belonged to the Boston Celtics and even though the St. Louis Hawks had good teams they could not consistently beat the Celtics. The Hawks did, however, beat them in 1958 and won the NBA Championship. Pettit scored 50 points in the final game.

◆ Pettit is the only player in NBA history to make the All-NBA team every year he was in the league. Only he and Jordan have averaged over 20 points a game every season they played. (LeBron and Kevin Durant have done that every year so far in their career.)

GEORGE MIKAN

Center | 6'10" | 1948-1956

Games	Pts (Avg)	TRB	Assist	FG%	FG3%	FT%
439	23.1	13.4	2.8	.402	NA	.782

4xAll Star, 6xAll-BAA/NBA, 3xScoring Champion, 5xBasketball Association of America/NBA Champion, 75th Anniversary NBA Team, Hall of Fame

George Mikan has the fewest professional games and the shortest career of any of the 75 players on my list. But only Wilt Chamberlain was responsible for changing more basketball rules then Mikan. Mikan the first truly "big man" in the NBA was responsible for the widening of the foul lane, introduction of goaltending violation, and the creation of the shot clock. He was most noted for his unstoppable hook shot with either hand and his outstanding underhanded free throw shooting. In the early years it was almost impossible for an offensive player to get a shot off on the inside with Mikan hovering around the basket. Mikan only played in the NBA seven years, but his Minnesota Lakers won 5 championships. In four of those championship series Mikan averaged 27.5 points and 14.1 rebounds. In the 1951 NBA Division Finals, which was the only one the Lakers lost while Mikan was playing, Mikan played with a fractured leg and still averaged 23 points. Although Mikan's career was short, he is currently 26th all-time in scoring average with a 23.1 average and 9th all-time in playoff rebound average with 13.9. Mikan averaged 23 points a game in an era with no shot clock and the average team in the NBA averaged 80 points. A great career for a kid that was told by the coach at Notre Dame, where he wanted to go, that he was too slow and awkward to ever be a basketball player. At the end of my coaching career in 2002 I was still teaching all my players the "Mikan Drill". A drill used to help players shoot around the basket with either hand, while keeping the ball above their shoulders.

❖ Mikan was voted the best player of the first half of the 20th Century.

ELVIN HAYES

Power Forward/Center | 6'9" | 1968-1985

Games	Pts (Avg)	TRB	Assist	FG%	FG3%	FT%
1303	21.0	12.5	1.8	.452	.147	.670

12xAll Star, 6xAll-NBA, 2xAll-Defensive Team, 1xNBA Champion, 2xTrb Champion, 1xNBA Champion, 1xScoring Champion, All-Rookie Team, 75th Anniversary NBA Team, Hall of Fame

Elvin "Big E" Hayes was the first pick of the San Diego Rockets in 1968. He began his phenomenal career by leading the NBA, as a rookie, in scoring with a 28.4 average and grabbing 17.1 rebounds. Hayes in his 16-year NBA career played with four different teams. His 1977-78 Washington Bullets team won the NBA Championship by beating the Supersonics in seven games. He averaged 21.8 points in the playoffs and led the playoffs with a 13.3 rebound average. Hayes led all scorers with 457 points in the playoffs that year. He finished his career with 27,313 points, currently 11th all-time and 16,279 rebounds, which is currently 6th all-time. Hayes is one of only seven players to have a scoring and rebounding title in his career. Elvin Hayes was a great college and NBA player, but I believe many basketball fans do not appreciate just how good Big E was.

 Hayes had 10 seasons averaging over 20 points a game and over 10 rebounds.

PATRICK EWING

Center | 7'0" | 1985-2002

Games	Pts (Avg)	TRB	Assist	FG%	FG3%	FT%
1183	21.0	9.8	1.9	.504	.152	.740

11xAll Star, 7xAll-NBA, ROY, 3xAll-Defensive Team, 75th Anniversary NBA Team, Hall of Fame

Patrick Ewing was the first player taken in the 1985 draft. He came out of Georgetown with a franchise tag and lived up to those expectations. In his first season with the Knicks, he averaged 20 points and nine rebounds. He made the NBA All Star team and was rookie of the year. Known throughout his career as a physical, tough inside post player Ewing averaged 2.4 blocks a game for his career. He averaged over 20 points and 2 blocks a game for 13 years in a row. (Olajuwon is the only other player to do this.) He also had a season where he averaged 28 points, 10 rebounds and 4 blocks. (No one else has done that.) Fifteen of Ewing's 17 years in the NBA were spent in New York where he led them to 13 playoffs. Ewing finished in the top 10 in the MVP voting seven times. Led by Ewing the Knicks returned to the Reed/Frazier glory days during the 1993-94 season when they went 62-20 but lost to the Houston Rockets in the NBA Finals. Ewing set a record for the most blocked shots in a Final's series with 30. He averaged 22 points and 11.7 rebounds for the playoffs. Ewing is currently 24th all-time in career points with 24,815 points, 25th with 11,607 rebounds, and 7th all-time in blocks with 2,894. Ewing is one of 6 players in the history of the NBA with 20,000 points, 10,000 rebounds and 2,500 blocks.

The gem for Ewing is a mixed blessing in that he never won a league MVP. He finished in the top 5 in voting 6 times, but he was a victim of position and era. Ewing is considered one of the best players of the decade of the 90s. Only 6 centers have made more All-Star teams!

CHARLES BARKLEY

Small Forward | 6'6" | 1984-2000

Games	Pts (Avg)	TRB	Assist	FG%	FG3%	FT%
1073`	22.1	11.7	3.9	.541	.266	.735

11xAll Star, 11xAll-NBA, 1xTrb Champion, All-Rookie Team, 1xNBA MVP, 75th Anniversary NBA Team, Hall of Fame

"Chuck" was one of the best rebounders to ever play in the NBA despite his 6'6" height. (He was probably closer to 6'5".) He made up for his height with his great leaping ability and his 250-pound frame. "The Round Mound of Rebound" led the league in rebounding in 1986-87 and is currently ranked as the 19th best rebounder of all time. Charles has the most 10 rebound seasons in NBA history with 15. He is the only player in NBA history to finish their career with over 20,000 points, 10,000 rebounds, 4,000 assists, 1,500 steals and a field goal average over 54%. Barkley is currently 27th all-time in scoring with 23,757 points. Charles Barkley known off the court as a humorous and good-natured personality could be very confrontational and combative on the court. He won the league MVP in 1992-93 and finished in the top six vote getters seven other seasons.

Barkley scored 56 points in a playoff game, which is the 4th highest in NBA history. Despite his 23 points and 12.9 rebounds per game average in the playoffs he never won an NBA Championship.

KARL MALONE

Power Forward | 6'9" | 1985-2004

Games	Pts (Avg)	TRB	Assist	FG%	FG3%	FT%
1476	25.0	10.1	3.6	.516	.274	.742

14xAll Star, 14xAll-NBA, 4xAll-Defensive Team, 2xNBA MVP, All-Rookie Team, 75th Anniversary NBA Team, Hall of Fame

"The Mailman" didn't deliver the mail but on the basketball court Karl Malone delivered everything else, points, rebounds, assists, and defense. Malone was as complete and as consistent a player to ever play in the NBA and he performed at that remarkable level for 19 years. The only two years Malone didn't average over 20 points was his first year and his last year in the NBA. The 17 years in between he was throwing up numbers like 27, 29, 31 points a contest and 11 to 12 rebounds per contest. Malone led the decade of the 90s in scoring. He had 17 seasons where he averaged more than 20 points a game. (Jabbar also had 17 and LeBron with 19 are the most.) He also led the league in games played five times, a testament to his consistency and durability. The Utah Jazz who drafted Malone in 1985 made the playoffs all 18 years he played for them. His playoff stats are identical to the regular season stats which reflects on his ability to play under pressure. Malone, along with John Stockton, led the Jazz to back-to-back NBA Finals in 1997 in 1998 losing both years to Jordan and the Bulls. In addition to being named the league MVP twice he finished in the top 10 in voting 14 times. Teaming with Stockton and perfecting the "screen and roll", Malone and Stockton are in a select company making up one of the most dynamic duos to ever play on the same team. Malone is currently 3rd all-time in points with 36,928 and 7th all-time in rebounds with 14,968. Malone also finished with 2,085 steals, currently 12th on the all-time list. He finished his career with the Lakers hoping to capture that elusive NBA championship but suffered a knee injury that ended his illustrious career and his championship dream. Despite Malone never winning an NBA title he has a career winning percentage of .645 (952-524). That is currently 5th all-time in wins in the history of the NBA.

One of only two players in NBA history to have over 30,000 points, 10,000 rebounds, 5,000 assists, 2,000 steals, and 1000 blocks. (LeBron is the other player.)

DAVID ROBINSON

Center | 7'1" | 1989-2003

Games	Pts (Avg)	TRB	Assist	FG%	FG3%	FT%
987	21.1	10.6	2.5	.518	.250	.736

10xAll Star, 10xAll-NBA, 1xScoring Champion, 1xTrb Champion, 1xBlk Champion, 2xNBA Champion, 8xAll-Defensive, ROY, 1xDef POY, 1xNBA MVP, 75th Anniversary NBA Team, Hall of Fame

David Robinson was the overall #1 draft pick in 1987 but did not join the San Antonio Spurs until 1989 because of his military obligation. The first year he played with the Spurs they won 35 more games than the year before he got there. (Biggest win differential at the time in NBA history.) "The Admiral" played his entire 14-year career with the Spurs. Robinson is #1 all-time for centers with the most seasons being named First Team All-NBA, and First Team All-Defensive in the same season with four. He led the Spurs to 12 playoffs and two championships in 1999 and 2003. Robinson's NBA achievements look like a best of the best list with championships in defense, scoring, rebounds and team championships. Robinson finished in the top 10 in MVP voting 8 times. He won the MVP award in 1994-95. He is currently 42nd on the career scoring list with 20,790 points, 32nd in rebounds with 10,497, and 6th all-time with 2,954 blocks. He and Jabbar are the only players in NBA history to win scoring, rebounding, and block shot titles during their career. He is one of only four players to record a quadruple double in a game.

❖ Robinson and Olajuwon are the only players in NBA history to have career averages of 20 points, 10 rebounds, and 3 blocks.

KEVIN GARNETT

Power Forward/Small Forward | 6'11" | 1995-2016

Games	Pts (Avg)	TRB	Assist	FG%	FG3%	FT%
1462	17.8	10.0	3.7	.497	.275	.789

15xAll Star, 9xAll-NBA, 1xNBA Champion, 12xAll-Defensive Team, 1xNBA MVP, All-Rookie Team, 4xTrb Champion, 1xDef POY, 75th Anniversary NBA Team, Hall of Fame

One of the first players mentioned in NBA laurels of players that went directly from high school to the NBA and were successful is Kevin Garnett. Drafted number five overall out of Farragut Academy as a 19-year-old Garnett averaged 10.4 points and 6.3 rebounds his first year in the NBA. Twenty-one years later, 1,462 games, 26,071 points, 1,859 steals and an NBA championship Garnett finished his career in the Hall of Fame. Garnett led the league in rebounding for four years and averaged 20.5 points in his first 12 years with the Minnesota Timberwolves, the team that drafted him. Only Tim Duncan with 15 has made more All-Defensive teams than Garnett's 12. (Kobe also has made the All-Defensive team 12 times.) His 2008 Celtic team which included Allen and Pierce defeated Kobe and the Lakers in the finals 4-2. Garnett is the only player in NBA history with 20,000 points, 10,000 rebounds, 5,000 assists, 1,500 steals, and 1,500 blocks. That is the definition of a complete player. When you combine All-NBA and All-Defensive selections Garnett has 21. (Only Jabbar, Duncan, and Kobe have more.)

❖ To illustrate just how complete a player Garnett was he finished his career with;26,071 points (18th), 14,662 rebounds (9th), 5,445 assists (52nd), 1,859 steals (18th), and 2,037 blocks (18th)

STEPHEN CURRY

Point Guard | 6'2" | 2009-Present

Games	Pts (Avg)	TRB	Assist	FG%	FG3%	FT%
826	24.3	4.6	6.5	.473	.428	.908

**8xAll Star, 8xAll-NBA, 2xScoring Champion, 4xNBA Champion,
All-Rookie Team, 2xNBA MVP, 1xFinals MVP,
75th Anniversary NBA Team**

Stephen Curry, like George Mikan and Wilt Chamberlain, has done more to revolutionize the way basketball is played than any other player in NBA history. Curry came into the league as a great three-point shooter and has taken his game to a higher level. Thousands of coaches at all levels, changed the way they taught offense and ran their fast break because of Curry and the three-point line. Curry is the #1 all-time 3-point shooter with 3117. He is 1 of 9 players in the 50/40/90 club. Curry led the Warriors to an NBA championship in 2015 with a 28.3 playoff scoring average. The Warriors also won the championship in 2017, 2018, and again last year. Curry averaged 28.1 in the 2017 series, 25.5 points in the 2018 series, and 27.4 in the 2022 playoffs. His playoff winning percentage of .694 is the 3rd best of all time for players who have played in a minimum of 100 games. His 2015-16 Golden State Warrior's team had the best regular season record of all time (73-9). Curry won back-to-back league MVPs in 2014-15 and 2015-16. He is a remarkable free throw shooter at 90.8 percent is currently number one all time among free throw shooters. No one in the history of the NBA has been able to shoot the ball at such a range as Curry with his accuracy. Of all the players who averaged over 20 points a game Curry is #2 all-time in Effective Field Goal

Percentage at .580. (Shaq is #1 at .582.) He is 9th among active players in scoring with 20,064 points.

💎 Curry is one of four players in NBA history to win multiple scoring titles, multiple MVPs and multiple championships. (Jabbar, Wilt and Jordan are the others.)

KEVIN DURANT

Small Forward/Power Forward | 6'10" | 2007-Present

Games	Pts (Avg)	TRB	Assist	FG%	FG3%	FT%
939	27.2	7.1	4.3	.496	.384	.884

12xAll Star, 10xAll-NBA, 4xScoring Champion, 2xNBA Champion, ROY, 1xNBA MVP, 2xFinals MVP, 75th Anniversary NBA Team

The Seattle Supersonics' made Kevin Durant the second player picked in the 2007 NBA draft. I'm sure the Portland Trail Blazers wish they had a do over. (They picked Greg Oden.) Durant is arguably the greatest shooter and offensive player to ever play in the NBA. At 6'10" Durant is impossible to stop outside by a big defender and can take a smaller defender to the basket. Durant averaged 20.3 points a game his first year in the NBA. He is the youngest scoring champion in NBA history. "KD" is 1 of 9 players in the 50/40/90 club and the youngest. Fifteen years after his league debut he is still scoring at a 29.9 clip and has led the NBA in scoring four times. Durant's teams have played in 11 playoffs where he has averaged 29.4 points a game. (Only Jordan and Iverson have a better playoff average.) The Golden State Warriors won back-to-back NBA championships in 2017 and 2018. Durant was named Finals MVP both years. (Only 12 players have won the award more than once.) KD has won the league MVP one time, in 2013-14, and has finished in the top 10 nine other times. He is third among active players in all-time scoring with 25,176 points and 14th among active players in rebounding with 6,556. Durant has scored over 25 points a game in 13 seasons. (Only LeBron with 18 has more.) He has won 3 Olympic gold medals and is Team USA's all- time leading scorer.

❖ Durant has averaged 20 points a game in every year he has played in the NBA. Only Pettit and Jordan have done that. LeBron has also done this so far in his career.

MOSES MALONE

Center | 6'10" | 1975-1995

Games	Pts (Avg)	TRB	Assist	FG%	FG3%	FT%
1455	20.3	12.3	1.3	.495	.096	.760

13xAll Star, 8xAll-NBA, 6xTrb Champion, 1xFinals MVP,
1xNBA Champion, 2xAll-Defensive Team, 3xNBA MVP,
ABA All-Time Team, 75th Anniversary NBA Team, Hall of Fame

Moses Malone was drafted by the Utah stars of the ABA as a 19-year-old from Petersburg, VA. He was the first player to ever go directly from high school to the pros. Only LeBron and Kobe had greater careers in the NBA of those players that went from high school into the pros. Malone in his first year averaged 18.8 points and 14.6 rebounds with the Stars. Nicknamed "The Chairman of the Board" because of his dominance on the inside and his tremendous rebounding ability. He led the NBA six times in rebounding including an amazing 17.6 rebounds per contest in 1978-79 with the Houston Rockets. Malone is recognized as the best offensive rebounder to ever play in the NBA. Some NBA fans say he missed shots so he could get his own rebound. He finished his career first on the all-time list in offensive rebounds with 6,731. (Parish is second with 4,598.) Malone won the NBA MVP award three times and finished in the top 10 seven other times. Charles Barkley gives Malone credit for teaching him and modeling for him how to work hard to be a great pro. He is currently 10th all-time in points with 27,409 and 3rd all-time with 17,834 rebounds. Malone made 13 All-Star teams and 8 All-NBA teams.

Malone had 11 seasons that he averaged over 20 points and over 10 rebounds a game. (5th all-time)

JERRY WEST

Point Guard/Shooting Guard | 6'3" | 1960-1974

Games	Pts (Avg)	TRB	Asist	FG%	FG3%	FT%
932	27.0	5.8	6.7	.474	NA	.814

14xAll Star, 12XAll-NBA, 1xScoring Champion, 1xAst Champion, 1xNBA Champion, 1x Finals MVP, 5xAll-Defensive Team, 75th Anniversary NBA Team, Hall of Fame

There is perhaps no other player from the pre-3-point era that would have benefited more than Jerry West. He was a great jump shooter with exceptional range. West and Oscar Robertson were considered the two best guards in the NBA in the decade of the 1960s. They came into the league as the number one and number two draft picks in 1960. Robertson the number one pick by the Cincinnati Royals and West the number two pick by the Los Angeles Lakers. West spent his entire 14 year playing career with the Lakers. After his first year West never averaged fewer than 20 points a game and led the NBA in scoring in 1969-70 with a 31.2-point average. Besides the NBA logo, West is known in the NBA as "Mr. Clutch". In 11 playoffs he averaged over 29 points and led the Lakers four times with an average of over 33 points. In the 1965 playoffs he averaged over 40 points a game. West is the only player in the history of the NBA to be named the MVP of the Finals even though his team lost to the Celtics. West is the all-time leading scorer in NBA Finals history with 1679 points and is third in assists. He finished in the top 6 in the MVP voting 9 times, but never won the award. In 1971 Chamberlain joined West in LA and got them to the promised land by beating the New York Knicks 4-1 in the NBA Finals. West led the NBA in a lot of categories but the one

The G.O.A.T – *The Quest to Find the Best*

he would have preferred to pass on was broken noses. He suffered 9 broken noses to go along with several injuries he suffered due to his hustle and relenting style of play. West is currently 22nd all-time with 25,192 points, and 34th with 6,238 assists. He was in the top 20 in field goal percentage in the league 10 times and in free throw percentage 11 times. It is said about Jerry West that he never gave up a possession, offensively or defensively, he played "all out". West was recognized as a great scorer and playmaker, but he made the all-defensive team 5 times even though the NBA did not start choosing all-defensive teams until West was in his 9th season. West made the All-Star team every year he played and made All-NBA 12 times. (Only 6 players have more All-NBA team selections.) The biggest question about West's career will never be answered; How many points would he have scored if there would have been a three-point line when he played?

❖ West, like Robertson, was a complete basketball player. They came into the league together and were compared and associated together much like Bird and Magic. West is recognized as one of the greatest players to ever play in pressure situations. "MR. CLUTCH" and "MR. LOGO"

110

JULIUS "DR.J" ERVING

Small Forward | 6'7" | 1971-1987

Games	Pts (Avg)	TRB	Assist	FG%	FG3%	FT%
1243	24.2	8.5	4.2	.506	.298	.777

16xAll Star, 7xAll-NBA, 1xNBA Champion, 2xABA Champion, 5xAll-ABA, 1xNBA MVP, 3xABA MVP, All-Rookie Team, 1xAll-Defensive Team, ABA All-Time Team, 75th Anniversary NBA Team, Hall of Fame

Dr. J, as the commercial says, was so good he became a doctor without going to medical school. In Erving's first year in the ABA with the Virginia Squires he averaged 27.3 points, 15.7 rebounds, and 4.0 assists. Dr. J's most iconic offensive move was his ability to drive to the basket and hang in the air until the defender came down before he shot the ball. Erving played five years in the ABA and was the MVP three times and finished second one other year. His ABA average is a remarkable 28.7 points and 12 rebounds a game. He led the New York Nets to the championship in 1974 and again in 1976. He averaged over 34 points a game in the 1976 playoffs. He is the best player to ever play in the ABA. Dr. J teamed up with Moses Malone, Maurice Cheeks, Bobby Jones, and Andrew Toney to win the NBA championship in 1982-83 with the Philadelphia 76ers. Many NBA followers have this team in the top 5 of all-time NBA teams. Erving's career record is 815-428 (.655). In his professional career (ABA/NBA) Erving scored 30,026 points and grabbed 10,525 rebounds. (35th currently) He is 1 of only 8 players to score over 30,000 points. Dr. J is one of four players to make the All-Star team in every year he played, and he did it for 16 years. He won four MVPs. (Only 6 players have won 4 or more.)

Erving and Garnett are the only players in professional basketball history to have 20,000 points, 10,000 rebounds, 5,000 assists, 1,500 steals, and 1,500 blocks.

BILL RUSSELL

Center | 6'10" |1956-1969

Games	Pts (Avg)	TRB	Assist	FG%	FG3%	FT%
963	15.1	22.5	4.3	.440	NA	.561

12xAll Star, 11xAll-NBA, 11xNBA Champions, 4xTrb Champion, 5xNBA MVP, 1xAll-Defensive Team, 75th Anniversary NBA Team, Hall of Fame

Mention the name Bill Russell and the first thing that comes to a basketball fan's mind is championships. No one athlete in any team sport has won more championship rings than Bill Russell's eleven. "Russ" picked up right where he left off with the San Francisco University Dons winning back-to-back national championships in 1955 in 1956 his last two years in college. The Celtics won 11 championships in Russell's 13 years as the center on some of the greatest teams ever in the history of the NBA. Many of you who are reading this are wondering how I have Bill Russell ranked 12th on my all-time list. How could he not be rated in the top five or maybe even be the G.O.A.T.? Please allow me to explain and please look at the criteria that I have spelled out in this book on how I would go about naming the best of the best. Granted, if you're evaluating players solely based on the accomplishments of their TEAM it would be hard not to put Russell in the top five. However, I am evaluating players based on a much more extensive and inclusive criteria. One of the leading criterion is a player's dominance on BOTH ends of the court. Russell only dominated on the defensive end of the court. He was never a one or two option offensively in the Celtics scheme. There is no question that Russell played a very significant ROLE in the 11 championships, but he played with five players that made the basketball Hall of Fame: Bob Cousy, Tom Heinsohn, Sam Jones, Bill Sharman, and John Havlicek. There has never been another center or player surrounded with such great talent. In the 13 playoffs Russell played in he led the Celtics in scoring only once. Russell finished his career as the second leading rebounder of all time with 21,620 (Wilt had 23,924.) and with 14,522 points. "Russ" won 5 MVPs, which is tied with Jordan, and one behind Jabbar for most in NBA history. (Three of those years he won the MVP he was not First Team All-NBA.) He made 11 All NBA teams but only 3 First Team selections. He is the #1 all-time career playoffs rebound leader with a 24.9 average. Obviously, I think Russell was a great player or I would not have him #12, but I think Bill Russell was the beneficiary of having great players around him, having a legend for a coach, and playing in an era when there were only 8 teams in the league.

Russell has the 8th best winning percentage of all-time when you combine the regular season and the playoffs (.707). Four Celtics have better percentages (KC Jones, Sam Jones, Tom Heinsohn, Larry Bird).

KOBE BRYANT

Shooting Guard/Small Forward | 6'6" | 1996-2016

Games	Pts (Avg)	TRB	Assist	FG%	FG3%	FT%
1346	25.0	5.2	4.7	.447	.329	.837

18xAll Star, 15xAll-NBA, 2xScoring Champion, 12xAll-Defensive Team, 5xNBA Champion, 1xNBA MVP, 2xFinals MVP, All-Rookie Team, 75th Anniversary NBA Team, Hall of Fame

Kobe Bryant was a first-round draft pick of the Los Angeles Lakers in 1996. "Black Mamba", as he liked to be called, was only 18 years old when he began his 20-year career, all with the Lakers. Only LeBron James has had a better career as an NBA player that came straight from high school into the league. When Shaquille O'Neal joined the Lakers in 1996, he and Kobe formed the league's best inside/outside duo and won NBA titles three straight years, 2000, 2001, and 2002. After Shaq left for Miami, Kobe along with Paul Gasol, Derek Fisher, Lamar Odom and HOF coach Phil Jackson won two more championships. Kobe only missed two all-star appearances in his twenty years in the league. He was in the top ten in the MVP voting 12 times and won the award once. His 18 All-Star appearances are second only to Jabbar. He was named MVP of the All-Star game 4 times, tied with Pettit for the most. Bryant came into the league and like most other players modeled his game after Michael Jordan. Bryant liked the comparison to Jordan and at the end of his career he thought he had reached equal status. MJ was the yardstick used by many NBA experts in evaluating the new players coming into the league. Bryant, who was taken much too young from us, has cemented his place in NBA basketball laurel. His 33,643 career points is currently 4th all-time; his 6,306 assists are currently ranked 33rd, and his 1,944 steals is currently 16th all-time. Kobe ranks 1st in career points, and rebounds, and is 2nd in assists by a shooting guard to Harden. Only Tim Duncan with 15 has made the All-Defensive Team more than Bryant and Garnett's 12. Like Jordan, Kobe Bryant played his best when his best was required. He had 8 career buzzer beaters, second to Jordan's 9. He finished 10th all-time in career wins with 836-510 and 9th all-time with 135 playoff wins. Dirk Nowitzki said it best when he said that both Jordan and Kobe had that "killer instinct". That would have brought a smile to Black Mamba's face. Kobe came up with this nickname for himself as an alter ego that was inspired by a code name of an assassin in the film Kill Bill.

❖ Kobe and LeBron are the only two players in NBA history with 30,000 points, 6,000 rebounds, and 6,000 assists.

OSCAR ROBERTSON

Point Guard | 6'5" | 1960-1974

Games	Pts (Avg)	TRB	Assist	FG%	FG3%	FT%
1040	25.7	7.5	9.5	.485	NA	.838

12xAll Star, 11xAll-NBA, 6xAst Champion, 1xNBA Champion, ROY, 1xNBA MVP, 75th Anniversary NBA Team, Hall of Fame

The "Big O" was the consummate basketball player. There wasn't anything that Robertson could not do on the basketball court and do extremely well. I saw Robertson play on my black and white TV back in 1959 when my local TV station in Illinois televised the Indiana high school state tournament. The Indiana State champions that year was an all-black school from Indianapolis, Crispus Attucks, led by Oscar Robertson. His team won back-to-back state championships. He capped off a great high school career by going undefeated in 45 straight games. After a great college career at the University of Cincinnati, the Cincinnati Royals made Robertson the number one pick in the 1960 draft. In his first year as a Royal he averaged 30.5 points, 10.1 rebounds, and 9.7 assists, razor close to a triple double. He is 1 of only 9 players in the history of the NBA to make All-NBA as a rookie. The following year he did average a triple double; 30.8 points, 12.5 rebounds, and 11.4 assists. The Big O went on to average a triple double his next five years in the NBA. In 1970 Robertson was traded to the Milwaukee Bucks where he joined another one of the NBA's all-time best, Lew Alcindor (Kareem Abdul-Jabbar). The Bucks went 66-16 that year and dominated everyone in the playoffs (12-2) to win the NBA title. Most NBA fans from that era remember the Big O for his ability to back smaller players down and score on a mid-range jumper. Robertson was considered a big guard and was as adept a passer as he was shooter. He led the league seven times in assists and is currently ranked 8th all-time with 9,887 assists, an average of 9.5 per game. He is one of three players in NBA history to average 30 points a game and 10 assists a game. He did it 5 times. (Nate Archibald and Westbrook did it once.) Robertson is currently 13th all-time with 26,710 points and 76th all-time with 7,804 rebounds. Oscar only won one league MVP but that was because in his era the MVP award usually went to a player on the team with the best record. Although he only won the award one time, he finished in the top 5 nine times. Finally, full disclosure before I finish this bio on the Big O. When I was playing basketball in high school in the early 60s, I would watch Oscar and try to copy his style, even shooting free throws with one hand. Then I realized there was only one Oscar Robertson.

❁ Oscar was a great pro the first time he stepped on the court in the NBA. He was First Team All-NBA in his first 9 years and averaged 30.3 points, 10.4 rebounds, and 10.6 assists in his first 5 years.

TIM DUNCAN

Power Forward/Center | 6'11" | 1997-2016

Games	Pts (Avg)	TRB	Asist	FG%	FG3%	FT%
1392	19.0	10.8	3.0	.506	.179	.696

15xAll Star, 15xAll-NBA, 5xNBA Champions, 15xAll-Defensive Team, ROY, 3xFinals MVP, 75th Anniversary NBA Team, Hall of Fame

Tim Duncan was the first pick in the 1997 NBA draft by the San Antonio Spurs and went on to play his entire 19-year career with them. The Spurs won 36 more games Duncan's rookie season than the year before he got there. He teamed up with David Robinson, Tony Parker, Manu Ginobili and Hall of Fame coach Greg Popovich to win 5 NBA titles. He didn't just play in five NBA Championship series he was the best player on each one of those teams. Duncan averaged 21.1 points and 11.9 rebounds his first year and made the NBA All-Defensive First Team. He was recognized around the league by the players and coaches as a stoic, unflappable and complete player that could beat you in several ways. NBA commissioner David Stern once described Duncan as a player for the ages. Duncan won two MVP's and finished in the top 10 eleven other seasons including finishing second twice. He made the All-Defensive Team 15 times of the 19 years that he played. (Most in history of NBA.) Duncan made the All-NBA team 15 times, only LeBron has more with 18. Duncan is currently 15th all-time with 26,496 points, 6th all-time with 15,091 rebounds, and 5th all-time with 3,020 blocks. He also played an unbelievable 47,368 minutes. (12th currently all-time) His career regular season record is 1001-391 (.719). (4th all-time)

◈ Tim Duncan never led the NBA in scoring, rebounding or blocked shots but finished his career in the top fifteen in all three categories. In the playoffs he finished his career #6 in scoring (5,172 points), #3 in rebounding (2,859 rebounds), and #1 in blocked shots (568 blocks).

HAKEEM OLAJUWON

Center | 7'0" | 1984-2002

Games	Pts (Avg)	TRB	Assist	FG%	FG3%	FT%
1238	21.8	11.1	2.5	.512	.202	.712

12xAll Star, 12xAll-NBA, 3xBlk Champion, 2xTrb Champion,
2xNBA Champion, 9xAll-Defensive Team, 2xDef POY,
All-Rookie Team, 2xFinals MVP, 1xNBA MVP,
75th Anniversary NBA Team, Hall of Fame

Hakeem "The Dream" Olajuwon was the first draft pick in the 1984 draft for a reason. He was a great player for the University of Houston Cougars, and an even better player for the Houston Rockets. Olajuwon, who is from Nigeria, is considered the best foreign player to ever play in the NBA. He is the first non-American player to be an All-star, an MVP and Defensive Player of the Year. In his first season he averaged 20.6 points, 11.9 rebounds, and 2.7 blocked shots. He led the league twice in rebounds and three times in blocks. In 14 playoffs with the Rockets, he averaged 26.6 points, 11.4 rebounds, and 3.3 blocks. He led the Rockets to back-to-back NBA championships in 1994 and 1995. He averaged 26.9 points in the 1994 finals and 32.8 points in the 1995 finals. Olajuwon set the standard (yardstick) for "footwork" among post players and even today NBA sports analysts compare the new players coming into the league with Olajuwon when it comes to their footwork and post moves. Olajuwon did not play basketball until he was 15 years old but excelled as a goalkeeper in soccer in his native Nigeria. Olajuwon won 1 MVP and finished in the top ten nine other times. He finished his 18-year career as the leading shot blocker in the history of the NBA with 3,830. He scored

26,946 points (currently 12th) and recorded 13,748 rebounds (currently 14th). He is one of only four NBA players to record a quadruple double in an NBA game; 18 points, 16 rebounds, 11 blocks, and 10 assists. He is the only player in NBA history to record 200 blocks and 200 steals in a season. The Dream made 12 All-Star teams and 12 All-NBA teams. (Shaq and Jabbar are the only centers to have more All-NBA selections.)

❖ Olajuwon finished his phenomenal 18-year career ranked in the top 15 in NBA history in scoring, rebounding, and blocked shots.

LARRY BIRD

Small Forward/Power Forward | 6'9" | 1978-1992

Games	Pts (Avg)	TRB	Assist	FG%	FG3%	FT%
897	24.3	10.0	6.3	.496	.376	.886

12xAll Star, 10xAll-NBA, 3xNBA Champion, ROY,
3xAll-Defensive Team, 2xFinals MVP, 3xNBA MVP,
75th Anniversary NBA Team, Hall of Fame

It is difficult to know where to start when you start writing about Larry Bird the basketball player. I will get to the stats and numbers later but first the thing that sticks out in my mind about Larry Bird is that he was so unassuming and yet so confident in his ability. He did not take himself too seriously but gave off this aura that he could kick anyone's butt on the basketball court. He and Magic Johnson rescued the NBA from obscurity in the decade of the 80s. It all began with the 1979 NCAA Final Four in Salt Lake City where they faced off for the first time of what would be many times. Ironically, their rivalry would develop into one of the greatest friendships off the court in all of sports. Magic's Michigan State team totally dominated Indiana State and Bird in the championship game 75-64. But to be fair to Bird, Magic had a lot better players around him. That game provided a glimpse of what was to come in the basketball world. I never saw them play, in person, in the NBA but that night on March 26th in the Special Events Center in Salt Lake City I had a seat about 20 rows up from the floor. The game remains a classic for Final Four Tournaments. If you read the first chapter of this book you will know what I mean by the "yardstick" test. For those of you who skipped that chapter to get right to the bios I explained my criteria for these picks. As a player or athlete in any sport if fans use a player to describe or define another that is what I call the yardstick. For example, "he's not as good a shooter as you fill in the blank". So, when describing a basketball player's ability to shoot the ball one often hears that XYZ cannot shoot the ball as good as Larry Bird. That is a great compliment. Taken a step further, you might hear that XYZ does not play under pressure as well as Larry Bird or for that matter Magic Johnson. That is what I call the yardstick. Larry Bird was a phenomenal basketball player for over 10 years until he started having issues with his back. The Boston Celtics won three titles with Bird leading the way. He won three MVPs in consecutive years and finished second four other times. Only Bird, Wilt, and Russell won the award three straight years. In Bird's rookie season the Celtics won 32 more games than in the previous year. He averaged over 20 points a game in his rookie season. Bird has always been a WINNER. He has the 2nd highest winning percentage of any player in NBA history at .735 (660-237). He is a member of the 50/40/90 club. Only he and Nash did it more than once. Bird is currently 36th all-time with 21,791 career points, 55th all-time with 8,974 rebounds, and 44th with 5,695 assists. His .886 free throw percentage is 13th all-time. The "Hick from French Lick" also led the league in another category not found in Basketball Reference but can be verified by asking the players he played against-- trash talking.

❀ Bird is the only player in NBA history to average 24 points, 10 rebounds, and 6 assists a game for their entire career.

SHAQUILLE O'NEAL

Center | 7'1" | 1992-2011

Games	Pts (Avg)	TRB	Assist	FG%	FG3%	FT%
1207	23.7	10.9	2.5	.582	.045	.527

15xAll Star, 14xAll-NBA, 2xScoring Champion, 4xNBA Champion, ROY, 3xAll-Defensive Team, 3xFinals MVP, 1xNBA MVP, 75th Anniversary NBA Team, Hall of Fame

Shaq was huge in every sense of the word, as a human being, as a personality, and certainly as a basketball player. Shaquille O'Neal has many nicknames but the one that perhaps fits him best is "Superman". The only thing that Superman could do that Shaq could not do is change clothes in a phone booth because Shaq could not get in one. He was the first pick in the 1992 draft by the Orlando Magic. In his first year he averaged 23.4 points, 13.9 rebounds, and 3.5 blocked shots. Shaq teamed up with Kobe Bryant to win three NBA titles with the Lakers from 2000 to 2002. In 2006 he joined Dwyane Wade with the Miami Heat to win a fourth title. He played in 6 NBA Finals and averaged 28.8 points, 13 rebounds and shot 60 % from the field. Shaq led the NBA in field goal percentage 10 times, the most in the history of the league. Ironically his field goal percentage for his career is higher than his free throw percentage. Shaq's best offensive move was to back or some might say bully the defender to the basket and then dunk the ball over him. He was impossible to stop when he got the ball in the lane close to the basket. One of the strategies that teams used to try to stop Shaq was to foul him before he could dunk the ball. That strategy even took on its own identity, "Hack-A-Shaq". In 14 playoff years from 1994-2007 Shaq averaged 25.5 points and 12.1 rebounds and was named the Finals MVP three times. From the year he entered the NBA until 2005 Shaq never finished lower than 9th in the regular season MVP voting. He was NBA MVP in 2000. One of the marks of a great player is winning with different team make-ups. Shaq won championships with two different franchises. His career record is 819-388. (.678) His playoff record is 129-87(.597) He is currently 8th all-time in career points with 28,596 points, 15th currently with 13,099 rebounds, and 8th all-time with 2,732 blocks.

Only 3 players in NBA history made more All-Star teams than Shaq and only 4 players made more All-NBA teams.

EARVIN "MAGIC" JOHNSON

Point Guard/Shooting Guard | 6'9" | 1979-1996

Games	Pts (Avg)	TRB	Assist	FG%	FG3%	FT%
906	19.5	7.2	11.2	.520	.303	.848

12xAll Star, 10xAll-NBA, 2xStl Champion, 4xAst Champion,
5xNBA Champion, All-Rookie Team, 3xNBA MVP, 3xFinals MVP,
75th Anniversary NBA Team, Hall of Fame

Magic is the quintessential name for Earvin Johnson, the basketball player. What he could do on a basketball court was truly magic. He was drafted first overall in 1979 and went to the perfect team, in the perfect city, a city that included Hollywood. Magic and his basketball talents were made for Hollywood and before his career ended, he received a lot of "Oscars". (NBA MVPs) Magic was the first 6'9" point guard but his legend grew while playing another position. He almost single-handedly won the 1980 NBA title with an unbelievable game six scoring 42 points and getting 15 rebounds, as the CENTER. Jabbar suffered an ankle injury with the Lakers ahead of the 76ers 3-2 in the Finals and could not play in Game 6. Magic announced to the team and the world "do not fear EJ is here". Promises backed up with results is what legends are made of i.e., Joe Namath, Muhammad Ali, Babe Ruth etc. In his first year in the NBA, he led the Lakers to the NBA Finals. He became the only rookie in NBA history to win Finals MVP. He scored 42 points, pulled down 15 rebounds, dished out 7 assists, while making 3 steals in game 6, the clinching game for the Lakers. Many NBA followers' rate that game as one of the best games in playoff history by any player. Magic spent his entire 13-year career as a Laker in the "City of Angels". He would have had even more remarkable stats if he hadn't sat out four years dealing with a new and scary illness, HIV. Magic led the NBA four times in assists. He also led the Lakers in the playoffs with a 12.3 assists average. He is the all-time career playoffs leader in assists. Magic was always at his greatest when the spotlight shined brightest. The Lakers won 5 NBA championships with Magic running the show. He also played in four other NBA Finals. He teamed with Jabbar to form one of the most imposing and dominating duos in all of basketball history. However, he is probably recognized as much for his link to a rival player from Boston. He and Larry Bird began there somewhat "friendly" rivalry in the NCAA tournament and carried on that "special" rivalry right on through their NBA careers. That rivalry and their extraordinary talent rescued the NBA from obscurity during the early 80s. Magic won three MVP's and finished second or third six other times. He finished his career with 17,707 points and 10,141 assists (currently 6th all-time.) Magic is considered the best point guard to ever play the game.

It has been difficult for me to try and chose just one particular, unique, and incredible stat on each one of these players that stands out above the rest, but that is not the case for Magic. He is the winningest player in the history of the NBA. His regular season winning percentage is .739 (670-236). His playoff record is 128-62 (.674). He won 5 championships and played in four other finals. Can you say WINNER!

WILT CHAMBERLAIN

Center | 7'1" | 1959-1973

Games	Pts (Avg)	TRB	Assist	FG%	FG3%	FT%
1045	30.1	22.9	4.4	.540	NA	.511

13xAll Star, 10xAll-NBA, 7xScoring Champion,
11xTRB Champion, 2xNBA Champion, 4xNBA MVP, ROY,
2xAll-Defensive Team, 1xFinals MVP, 75th Anniversary NBA Team,
Hall of Fame

Wilt Chamberlain was the most dominating basketball player of his generation and arguably the most dominating player to ever play the game. No other player has been responsible for so many rule changes to the game of basketball than Wilt Chamberlain i.e., free throw lane, free throw shooting, goal tending, etc. Like Jabbar, Chamberlain could not enter the NBA as a teenager right out of high school but began his NBA career in 1959 at the age of 23. That is truly significant in sports when your youth and physicality are so important. Obviously, your body is your greatest asset as an athlete. Those athletes who participate in sports like hockey, tennis, baseball and basketball at an early age are the ones who typically end up in the Hall of Fame. In Chamberlain's first year in the league, he led the league in points with a 37.6 average, rebounds with a 27.0 average, and minutes played. It would seem perfectly rational to me to think he could have put up similar numbers as a 19 or 20-year-old. "The Big Dipper", his favorite nickname, led the league in points seven times including a record 50.4 points per game in 1961-62, a record that still stands. He led the league in rebounds 11 times including an average of over 27 in 1959-60 and 1960-61. In his first playoffs he averaged 33.2 points and 25.8 rebounds. In his 14 seasons he led the league 9 times in minutes per game played. Wilt had 124 30/30 games in his career, all other NBA players COMBINED have had 32. Chamberlain holds many firsts or only in the NBA; only player to average 50 points a game, only player to score 100 points in a game, only center to lead the league in assists (He did that in response to sports writers accusing him of shooting too much and not being able to pass.) Wilt is the only player to average 30 points and 20 rebounds for a season, only player to get 2,000 rebounds in one season (2,149), only player to score over 4,000 points in season (4,029). Chamberlain finished his career with 31,419 points which is currently 7th all-time, 23,924 rebounds (currently 1st all-time), and 4,643 assists (81st currently all-time). Neither Wilt nor Russell played in the NBA when blocked shots were kept. (They would have likely finished #1 and #2 in that category.) The only two criticisms that are ever made about Chamberlain when he played in the NBA were; he only won two NBA titles, and he could not shoot free throws. Only one of these criticisms is fair and has merit, he could not shoot free throws. As for the other criticism that he did not win but two championships, basketball is a team game. Chamberlain never had great players as teammates except for a few years. No matter how much fluff and rhetoric is spouted about the matchup between Russell and Chamberlain, Wilt dominated their games. In 94 regular season games between the two Wilt averaged 29.9 points a game to Russell's 14.2. Wilt averaged 28.1 rebounds to Russell's 22.9. Assists were even but in field goal percentage it was .488 Wilt to .370 Russell. Russell had the edge in free throw percentage but neither one of them were very good. (Russell .543 to Wilt .488) In the playoffs the numbers were about the same with Wilt averaging 25.7 points to Russell's 14.9. Wilt averaged 28.0 rebounds to Russell's 24.7. But in field goal percentage in the playoffs Chamberlain's FG% went up to .508 and Russell's was .417. I know all about the wins and losses argument, I grew up in that era and saw it for myself. I have always said that if Wilt and Russ would have switched teams the records would have been the same OR perhaps the Celtics might have NEVER lost a championship. Russell said, "Wilt Chamberlain was the most athletic player to EVER play in the NBA". They say that records are meant to be broken but I think Wilt Chamberlain set records in the NBA that will never be broken. He still holds 72 NBA records, and he retired over 50 years ago! Wilt won four NBA MVPs but for some inexplicable reason he DID NOT win the award the year he averaged 50 points and 25 rebounds. (Russell did.)

I could have devoted an entire chapter to Wilt Chamberlain's basketball records but if you are an NBA fan you already know that no one in the history of the game has come close to individually dominating the NBA to the extent that Wilt did. So how can Wilt not be the G.O.A.T.? When I started this book and the research several months ago, I thought he would be. I have always maintained that he was the greatest. What changed my mind? Longevity, the era in which he played and through no fault of his, the lack of championships. The NBA kept changing rules to try and neutralize his tremendous talent, but he still dominated the league like no one else ever has. I or any NBA savant could easily make an argument for Wilt to be the G.O.A.T.

MICHAEL JORDAN

Shooting Guard/Small Forward | 6'6" | 1984-2003

Games	Pts (Avg)	TRB	Assist	FG%	FG3%	FT%
1072	30.1	6.2	5.3	.497	.327	.835

14xAll Star, 11xAll-NBA, 10xScoring Champion, 6xNBA Champion, ROY, 9xAll-Defensive Team, 1xDefensive POY, 6xFinals MVP, 5xNBA MVP, 75th Anniversary NBA Team, Hall of Fame

Michael Jordan is one of the most recognized SPORTS names in the world. In a survey of the greatest athletes of all time Michael Jordan was voted number one. He was followed in that survey by #2 Muhammad Ali, #3 Wayne Gretzky, #4 Usain Bolt, #5 Babe Ruth, #6 Michael Phelps, #7 Tiger Woods, #8 Bo Jackson, #9 Pele, and #10 Roger Federer. LeBron James showed up at 12th on the list. This survey was conducted in 2010 and as they say "times have changed" or has it when it comes to picking the greatest basketball player of all time. Jordan has been considered the G.O.A.T. for several years and his popularity has not diminished much since his retirement almost 20 years ago. Among Jordan's many aliases he is referred to as "His Airness" and "Air Jordan", those two references get to the heart of what made Michael Jordan so special on the basketball court. There have been other basketball players with great leaping ability and hang time, but no other player was able to do the things with a basketball that Jordan did while defying gravity. There is much more to Jordan then just his legs. He has the heart of a champion, the focus of a sniper, the hands of a surgeon, the mind of an assassin, the will of a Secretariat, the discipline of Job and the determination and competitive spirit of, well,

Michael Jordan. Everyone wants to define greatness with stats and numbers, but it isn't that easy. All the players that you have read about in this book and many more who did not make the book have great numbers. The question, and it is a very difficult question to answer, is what sets one great player apart from another? MJ checks all the boxes to be the G.O.A.T.; dominance, longevity, the yardstick test, excels on offense and defense, team championships, excels under pressure(clutch), and finally the stats. Jordan was five-time league MVP. Only Jabbar with six has more. He also finished second and third five other times in the voting. His Chicago Bulls team won the NBA title six times. Jordan was the MVP all six times the Bulls won the championship. He led the league in scoring 10 times and has the all-time best career average at 30.12 just a half point better than Chamberlain. He and Pettit are the only two players in NBA history to average over 20 points every season of their career. He is currently 47th all-time in assists with 5,633 and 3rd in steals with 2,514. Jordan's ability to perform at a phenomenal level when the stakes were the highest is reflected in his 33.4 average in the playoffs, which is three points better than during the regular season. Jordan made the First Team All-NBA and First Team All-Defensive team in the same season 9 times, most of any player. His career won-loss record is 706-366 (.659). His playoff won-loss record is 119-60 (.664).

❖ Bird and Magic are rightly given credit for resurrecting the NBA in the early 80s. Jordan almost single-handedly took the league to another level in the 90s.

KAREEM ABDUL-JABBAR

Center | 7'2" | 1969-1989

Games	Pts (Avg)	TRB	Assist	FG%	FG3%	FT%
1560	24.6	11.2	3.6	.559	.056	.721

19xAll Star, 15xAll-NBA, 2xScoring Champion, 4xBlk Shots Champion, 1xTrb Champion, 11xAll-Defensive Team, ROY, 2xFinals MVP, 6xNBA MVP, 75th Anniversary NBA Team, Hall of Fame

Lew Alcindor could have been the number one pick in the 1965 draft as a 19-year-old high schooler coming out of Power Memorial High School in New York. The NBA was not drafting high school players back in 1969. His freshman UCLA team beat the UCLA #1 pre-season ranked varsity team in a scrimmage. But as we know Lew Alcindor became Kareem Abdul-Jabbar and became not just a great college player but an even better professional player. Bill Walton has said on many occasions that Jabbar was the best basketball player he ever saw. Like all the great ones Jabbar's stats can fill up a book and still not tell the true story of how great a basketball player he was. His first year in the NBA in 1969-70 he averaged 28.8 points a game and 14.5 rebounds. The NBA did not record block shots until Jabbar's fifth season in the league when he averaged 3.5, so it would be safe to assume he was blocking over three shots a game in those first four years in the league. While Jabbar's patented hook shot did not revolutionize the game like Chamberlain's offensive dominance, his hook shot was deadly and undefendable. His hook shot even took on its own identity, it was called the "Skyhook". Jabbar made more NBA All-Star Teams than anyone (19). He was selected to the All-NBA team 15 times, most by a center. He won more MVP's (6) than anyone who ever played. He and Robinson are the only players in NBA history to lead the league in scoring, rebounds and blocks. At 39 and 40 years of age he was performing at a high enough level to make and NBA All-Star team. In his first 12 years in the league, he averaged 28.1 points, 14.1 rebounds, 3.4 blocks, and shot and incredible 55.6% from the field. He also played in over 80 games every year except three. He did that for 12 years. In those same 12 years in the playoffs, he averaged 28.8 points, 14 rebounds, 3.4 blocks, and shot 53.6% from the field. Besides his six MVPs he finished in the top 10 eleven other times. He teamed with the Big O to win an NBA title in Milwaukee in 1971 before an amazing run of five NBA titles in the 80s with Magic and the Lakers. Jabbar is currently the number one all time points leader for a career with 38,387. He ranks #3 all-time in playoff points. Jabbar finished his career with 17,440 rebounds (currently ranked 3rd all-time). He finished his career with 3,189 blocks which is 3rd all-time even though the NBA did not keep that stat his first 4 years in the league. Jabbar is the only player in NBA history to lead the league in scoring, rebounding, blocks, and field goal percentage during their career. I can't help but wonder how many points Kareem Abdul-Jabbar might have ended up with had he had the opportunity to go directly into the NBA out of high school as so many players like LeBron were able to do. Jabbar was a great player and was great for a very very long time.

❖ At the time Jabbar retired in 1989 after an unbelievable 20-year career he was the all-time leader in: Points, Games, Minutes Played, Field Goals Made, Blocked Shots, Career Wins, Playoff Points, Finals Points, MVPs, All-NBA Selections, All-Star Selections.

LeBron James

Forward/Guard | 6'9" | 2003-Present

Games	Pts (Avg)	TRB	Assist	FG%	FG3%	FT%
1364	27.1	7.5	7.4	.505	.346	.734

18xAll Star, 18xAll-NBA, 1xAst Champion, 1xScoring Champion, 4xNBA Champion, ROY, 6xAll-Defensive Team, 4xNBA MVP, 4xFinals MVP, 75th Anniversary NBA Team

LeBron James may very well live up to one of his many nicknames, King James. No other player in the history of the NBA has come into the league and dominated for as long as James. King James is in his 19th year and at 37 years old finished this last season with a remarkable 30-point average. The seemingly unreachable all-time scoring record held by Kareem Abdul-Jabbar is in his sights, just 1,325 points away. His talents are surpassed by no one in the 75 years that the NBA has existed. Several sports media that is involved with the NBA has Jordan and James ranked #1 and #2 as the best to ever play the game. Many have James rated above Jordan. Basketball Reference list James's position as every position but center. His versatility and durability are unquestionable. He has made the All-Star team every year he has been in the league but his first year. As a 19-year-old rookie he averaged over 20 points and had almost six assists a game, numbers worthy of an All-Star selection. NBA analyst Brian Windhorst said of James "No one has ever had as much hype as James has had to live up to and James has delivered on every last drop". LeBron has the most All-NBA selections with 18 and the 2nd most All-Star selections with 18 of anyone in NBA history. (Jabbar has 19 All-Star appearances.) Only Jabbar, Jordan and Russell have more MVPs than LeBron. He has won four NBA championships and played in a total of 10 finals. (Only Russell and Sam Jones have played in more.) But unlike the other three players James has played in the finals with THREE different teams proving his impact on the team. On each one of the championship teams LeBron played a different position. (Small forward, power forward and shooting guard.) He has scored the most points of any player in the history of the playoffs with 7,631(28.7 avg). He has the most career playoff wins with 174. Only West has more points in the Finals than LeBron. (1,679 for West and 1,562 for LeBron) As mentioned, he is second all-time in total points with 37,062. He is currently 38th in career rebounds with 10,210, 7th in career assists with 10,045, 10th in steals with 2,136, and 11th in 3 pointers with 2,140. James has only missed being in the top 10 in the MVP voting two times. The fact that James was not in the top 10 in 2018-19 or again in 2020-21 is an anomaly. He averaged 27.4 points and 8.3 rebounds in the 2018-19 season and 25 points and 7.8 assists in the 2020-21 season. One of the reasons that James has had such a long and outstanding career is due to his discipline and the way he takes care of himself. That would also explain why he is third all-time in minutes played with 52,139 minutes.

❖ With one more healthy season LeBron will likely have more points than arguably the best center (Jabbar) of all-time and more assists than the best point guard of all-time (Magic).

THE G.O.A.T

So, there you have it, let the gnashing of teeth and the criticism began. I know that I have left off a lot of great players and probably one of your favorites. If you criticize this list without having first read my introduction and the first two chapters where I define my criteria, then shame on you. If I failed to follow my own criteria and guidelines, then shame on me. I tried to be as objective and as fair as humanly possible. My goal was not to please anyone but to be fair and follow the criteria wherever it led me. As I said in the first few pages of this book, this is an exercise in futility, but I have enjoyed the journey. I did take this exercise seriously. I am not going to apologize for anyone of these great players on my Top 75 list, they deserve to be there. It is always easy to say, "well I think so and so should have made the list, how could X or Y have been left off?" I think a better question would be who do you take off to replace him? Like any limited list it is hard to draw the line and it never seems fair to a team or a player that just misses or was next in line. I have to say that picking this list got harder as I got closer to the top and began to focus on the G.O.A.T. I even entertained the thought of not assigning a number to the top five but just let you the reader decide. That is not the way I operate, I'm not an everyone gets a trophy guy. Again, I tried to base my choices on a set of solid criteria, truths that I have adopted over 70 years of playing, coaching, and being a spectator of this great game. That elusive IT is hard to identify. However, I believe that if a person has been in the arena, they have a better understanding of what IT takes to be great.

Greatness is easy to recognize but sometimes hard to define. But after spending over 70 years of my life in sports here is what it boils down to. Who would you choose to begin a franchise with if you were an owner? Who would you choose to build a team around if you were the coach? Who would you choose as a teammate if you were playing for your first born, well maybe not that high of stakes, maybe just your house? Chamberlain, Kobe, Magic, Kareem, MJ, Shaq, LeBron or you might pick someone else that is not even on my all-decade teams. Remember I didn't say this was an experiment in science, there is a lot of subjective reasoning that went into this. I tried to stick to the criterion, but I didn't do this to try and convince anyone how smart I was or that I am right. I did spend several months reviewing, researching, and recalling, and again what I have been fortunate to see with my own eyes for seven decades. I also had a great friend who loves the NBA as much if not more than I do. He has followed the league and players religiously for over 40 years. He is an NBA savant. I have tried to remain open-minded and objective throughout this whole process. He has helped me stay true to my stated criterion. Up until a year ago I never thought about writing a book about the NBA and undertaking a project like this quest to recognize the best. I'm glad I did. I am excited to share my thoughts and outcomes with you. This is my second book so I should be able to say that this one was easier than *Welcome To My World* but truthfully it was a lot of work, and I had help with the research! My love for the game and my background as a player and coach has benefited me immensely. At heart I am a history buff and am constantly looking back to compare certain things and persons to the present. Sometimes I am encouraged by what I see and other times not so much. That applies to the game of basketball as well.

After all the lists, stats, anecdotes and some nostalgia I have a confession to make. I cannot finish this book with any kind of deception about the Top 75 or my choice as the G.O.A.T. My all-time favorite player is Jerry West. The player I always said, and thought was the greatest to ever play the game is Wilt Chamberlain. That was before I wrote this book. Putting aside my prejudices and sticking to the criteria that I laid out in detail in this book I have come to this conclusion; The basketball G.O.A.T. is LeBron Raymone James Sr. He checks all the boxes, in spades. It is so difficult and, in many ways, unfair to so many great players to name one as being better than another. I think I have made a good case for my Top 75 and why I ranked them where I did. LeBron is not perfect, but he is awfully close. He is the ultimate, complete basketball player. He can play all five positions. He can score. He can defend. He can rebound. He can handle the ball and pass. However, the determining factor for me was that LeBron James has won four NBA titles WITH THREE different teams while playing THREE different positions. The common DenOMINATOR on each of those teams, King James.

THE ALL-DECADE TEAMS

I have based my Top 75 list from my research and the information that I gathered from the all-decade teams. As I mentioned several times, I don't think it is possible to be considered one of the greatest players of ALL time if that player was not a great player of A time. (Each one of the players in the Top 75 were considered the best in the era they played.) It is much easier to pick great players within a particular era or time frame for several reasons. For the most part they (A) played head-to-head, (B) played under the same rules, (C) played according to how the game was called, (D) played on the same type of court (3-point line, lane, etc.) There is no denying the game has changed. It has evolved over the years in many ways. The most obvious and undeniable is the quality of and size of the participants. The skill, size and athleticism of the players is the best it has ever been since the league's first game in 1947. The NBA has grown in fame and stature. It is recognized all around the world as a universal game not just an American game. The proof is in the number of "foreign" players that are now playing in the league. They have brought a new dimension and skill set to the league. Until recently I never thought that I would see a dynasty again in the NBA like the Celtics of the 60s but with free agency and the "big market" teams seemingly trying to "corner" the talent that might happen. The reason I mentioned this was to remind everyone that this is a book about the players not necessarily the teams. Team achievement and winning is only one of the ten criterion that I used to select the best of the best players for the last 75 years. Playing for a particular franchise had no bearing on my selections. Again, this was not an exercise based on notoriety and fame.

It is an incredible honor to be chosen as an All-Decade player. To even play in the NBA for a decade is very difficult given all the new talent coming into the league every year. A player that excels for 10 years or in most cases longer in the NBA is a very special player. From these All-Decade teams I was able to focus on the special qualities that separates one player from another and thus arrive at the ultimate goal of choosing the G.O.A.T. Because there were only eight teams, for the most part in the 50s and 60s, I only picked 5 players for those decades. I chose 10 players to represent the decade of the 70s to present because of the number of teams and players in those decades.

THE 1950s:

#1. George Mikan
#2. Bob Pettit
#3. Bob Cousy
#4. Dolph Schayes
#5. Paul Arizin

The lane was widened from 6 to 12 feet in 1951 to try to lessen Mikan's dominance. The 24-second clock was implemented in 1954 to create a faster pace game and promote more scoring. Before the shot clock the average score was in the 70s and the average team field goal percentage was .375. The league was very unstable varying from 8 to 17 teams.

THE 1960s:

#1. Wilt Chamberlain
#2. Oscar Robertson
#3. Bill Russell
#4. Jerry West
#5. Elgin Baylor

❧ The league stabilized in the 60s with 8 teams before a 9ᵗʰ team (Chicago) was added in 1966. Chamberlain was the most dominating player, and the Celtics were the most dominating team of the 60s. Several rules were changed to try and neutralize Wilt's dominance; offensive goal tending, the lane was widened again from 12 feet to 16 feet, in bounds passes could not be thrown over the backboard to eliminate Wilt from just going up over everyone and dunking the ball, and a free throw shooter could not go over the foul line until the ball hit the basket so he could not basically throw the ball to himself. The 60s was the highest scoring decade in the history of the NBA. The average team score was between 118 points and 110. In 1966 the ABA came into existence.

THE 1970s:

#1. Kareem Abdul-Jabbar
#2. Julius Erving
#3. Elvin Hayes
#4. John Havlicek
#5. Rick Barry
#6. Walt Frazier
#7. George Gervin
#8. Willis Reed
#9. David Cowens
#10. Bob McAdoo

❧ The NBA went from 14 to 22 teams. The ABA and NBA merged in 1976 and the NBA benefited by adding the great Dr. J, Gervin, Barry and several other ABA players into the league. Jabbar was the dominating player in the 70s winning 6 MVPs and never finishing lower than fourth in the voting. Julius Erving came into the league after dominating the ABA with 3 MVPs and 2 ABA championships. Only the Celtics and the Knicks won more than one title in the 70s. They both won two.

THE 1980s:

#1. Magic Johnson
#2. Larry Bird
#3. Moses Malone
#4. Isiah Thomas
#5. James Worthy
#6. Kevin McHale
#7. Dominique Wilkins
#8. Robert Parish
#9. Alex English
#10. Adrian Dantley

❖ Larry Bird and Magic Johnson literally saved the NBA from obscurity. The game was played faster and more fluid before the hand-checking and the ugly, physical style of the Detroit Pistons took over in the mid to late 80s. The 1982 Milwaukee Bucks may have been the best NBA team to never win a championship. The draft lottery was introduced and so was the explosion of exposure via the cable networks. Along with the exposure came a huge increase in salaries for the players brought on in part by the huge deals the players received from the shoe companies. Bird and Magic led in that department, as well, until MJ showed up. The Celtics and the Lakers were once again the "dream" franchises of the 80s.

THE 1990s:

#1. Michael Jordan

#2. Shaquille O'Neal

#3. Hakeem Olajuwon

#4. David Robinson

#5. Karl Malone

#6. Charles Barkley

#7. Patrick Ewing

#8. Scottie Pippen

#9. Clyde Drexler

#10. Gary Payton

Michael Jordan and the Chicago Bulls pretty much sums up the decade of the 90s. They won 6 championships with Jordan and Pippen dominating. Jordan won 5 league MVPs and 6 NBA Finals MVPs. The Houston Rocket's capitalized on Jordan taking two years off to try his hand at baseball and won back-to-back NBA titles in 1994 and 1995. Hakeem "The Dream" established himself as one of the all-time NBA greats. Every decade had great players, but no decade had the depth and caliber of talent of the 90s.

THE 2000s:

#1. Tim Duncan

#2. Kobe Bryant

#3. Kevin Garnett

#4. Dirk Nowitzki

#5. Paul Pierce

#6. Steve Nash

#7. Allen Iverson

#8. Jason Kidd

#9. Tracy McGrady

#10. Ray Allen

❖ The NBA reverts to the mid-80s as a more physical, ugly style of play. The average team score was in the low 90s. The Laker's 3-peat before Shaq and Kobe break-up. Duncan and the Spurs won back-to-back championships. The most hyped rookie in the history of the league made his debut in 2003 in the person of LeBron James.

The 2010s:

#1. LeBron James

#2. Kevin Durant

#3. Stephen Curry

#4. Dwyane Wade

#5. Giannis Antetokounmpo

#6. James Harden

#7. Kawi Leonard

#8. Russell Westbrook

#9. Carmelo Anthony

#10. Dwight Howard

❖ Massive changes took place in the NBA due to the explosion of analytics of Darryl Morey, the GM of the Houston Rockets. He "figured out" that a team making only one-third of their 3s was the equivalent of a team that shoots 50% from inside the arc. The decade saw the domination of "The Chosen One", LeBron James, who won four championships with three different teams. Perhaps the most exciting player of the 2010s was Steph Curry and his assault on the 3-point line. Curry revolutionized the way the game was played with his ability to score from "Downtown". At the end of the decade of the 2000s the average team attempted 18 three pointers a game. Today the average team takes 35 three pointers a contest. Team offenses have been totally altered due to the 3-pointer and expounding on the "Morey" offensive scheme. Guards such as Curry and James Harden have a much greater impact on the outcome of the games.

As you have perused the all-decade teams, I am sure you have noticed that several players overlap decades in their playing days i.e., Jordan came into the league in 1984 but had his best years in the 90s. I tried to place the players in the decade that they played most of their games in or the decade where they received their most recognition. It was especially difficult to place Frazier, Havlicek, Barry and Westbrook. I chose the #1 player in each decade using the same criteria that I used to pick the Top 75. In some of the decades like the 1950s and 2000s it was hard to pick #1. The decade of the 90s was loaded! As I stated several times it is very difficult if not impossible to compare greatness in one decade with another. Picking all-decade teams does provide some insight into picking a Top 75 across all time periods.

Special Mention for Players
with Shortened Careers

As I promised there were some of the greatest basketball players of all time that did not make the Top 75 through no fault of their own. I wanted to acknowledge those players that came up short due to injuries that shortened their career. Most of these players were great and dominated this sport but just not for very long. Staying true to one of my primary criteria, longevity, I did not think that they deserved the recognition over the 75 that I have chosen. There have been several players throughout the history of the NBA that a fan just "wrings" their hands and thinks that poor guy can't stay healthy. Mickey Mantle was that way in baseball. You can't help but wonder what they could have done if they were able to play a whole season or 10 seasons in a row? I am not implying that all these players on my "bad luck" list would have made my Top 75 but some of them certainly would have. A player's health can sometimes be a fickle thing and regardless of whether the player does all the right things or not it just doesn't work out.

The first player that I want to recognize that was a victim of a short NBA career but was a great player is Bill Walton. Walton was one of the greatest college players of all time. I saw Bill Walton in the NCAA Finals in Saint Louis in 1973 when he was not only dominating but he was almost perfect. UCLA completely dominated Memphis State in the championship game and won 87-66. Walton scored 44 points, and only missed one field goal the entire game going 21 of 22 and grabbed 15 rebounds. That same year I had the privilege to see Walton up close when I attended one of UCLA's practices. I was an assistant coach at Oral Roberts University and Coach Wooden had extended an invitation to our head coach, Ken Trickey, to come out to LA and watch one of his practices. John Wooden was my coaching hero so to get to watch one of his practices and talk with him was very special. In nine NBA seasons Walton only played ONE full season (80 games). In 1976-77 with the Portland Trail Blazers, he played in 65 games and averaged 18.6 points and had a league best 14.4 rebounds. The Trail Blazers won the NBA championship that year and Walton was the Finals MVP. He played limited minutes in the 1986 playoffs averaging 7.9 points and 6.4 rebounds as a member of the Boston Celtics championship team. Bill Walton, when healthy, was as good as any center who has ever played the game.

Blake Griffin started, or should I say, didn't start his career in 2009 the year he was drafted #1 overall out of the University of Oklahoma. The first game he played for the Los Angeles Clippers was in 2010. Griffin was named ROY that year and averaged 22.5 points and 12.1 rebounds. He also made the first of six all-star teams and the first of five all NBA teams. In his first nine seasons he averaged 21.9 points and 9.0 rebounds. In three of those years, Griffin played fewer than 40 games. A highflier, Griffin only had three seasons when he played 80 games. However, in each one of those three seasons he averaged over 20 points and just under 10 rebounds a contest. He finished third in the voting for league MVP in 2013-14. Griffin is currently 19th among active players in points with 14,334 and 20th in rebounds with an 8.2 average.

Penny Hardaway was a phenomenal player in the NBA right from his first game in 1993. He was drafted by Golden State but at Shaq's request was traded to the Orlando Magic. In his second season with the Magic and playing with Shaq, the Magic won a franchise record 57 games. They were defeated in the finals by the champion Houston Rockets, but Hardaway averaged 25.5 points in the series that year. Hardaway averaged 20.9 points and 7.2 assists and was chosen to the All-NBA team and the All-Star team. After the third season with the Magic and with the departure of Shaq to the Lakers, Hardaway began having issues with his knee. During the 1997-98 season he missed most of the season after knee surgery. He never fully recovered from the knee issues. In the final ten years of his career, he was only able to play 60 or more games 3 seasons. The first six years of his career he averaged 18.7 points and 6.2 assists. The last eight years of his career he averaged 9.6 points and 3.2 assists. Hardaway made four All-Star teams and finished third one year in the MVP voting and 5th another year.

David Thompson was one of the best basketball players that I personally ever saw play. In 1974 I was an assistant coach at Oral Roberts university when we played Kansas in the finals of the Midwest regional for a chance to go to the Final Four. We lost in overtime and Kansas went on to play Marquette in the semifinals. In the other semifinal game North Carolina State beat UCLA 80-77 in two overtimes. Everyone covering the Final Four believed that the national championship game was played on Saturday between North Carolina State and UCLA. They were right. Two nights later North Carolina State beat Marquette 76-64 in the finals and UCLA beat Kansas by twenty for third place. On that NC State team was an All-American named David Thompson who scored 49 points and was named MVP of the tournament. During that same period, we had a player at ORU named Anthony Roberts who was a freshman on our team that year we almost made it to the Final Four. Roberts went on to make All American and get drafted in the first round by the Denver Nuggets, the same team that David Thompson was playing for. Thompson and Roberts played together for three years and became close friends. So how is this relevant to the Top 75? I can tell you that from up close and a personal experience David Thompson was great. Many basketball fans may not have even heard of "Skywalker". If he had started his career in the NBA instead of the ABA and stayed healthy, he could have been in the top 50. In nine years in the

NBA/ABA he averaged 22.7 points and made five all-star teams. He was ROY in the ABA and made the ABA all-time team. At 6'4" he had unbelievable leaping ability and was impossible to guard.

Yao Ming was 7'6" and for 8 seasons he was truly "The Great Wall". The Houston Rockets made Ming their first pick in the 2002 draft. He made the All-Star team every year he was in the NBA. Ming was a five time all NBA selection and was voted into the Hall of Fame. He averaged 19 points and 9.2 rebounds in his shortened 486 game career. In four playoff series he averaged 19.8 points and 9.3 rebounds.

Derrick Rose was the first overall pick in the 2008 draft by the Chicago Bulls. As a 20-year-old in his first year in the league he averaged 16.8 points and six assists. At 21-years-old, in only his second year in the league, he averaged 20.8 points, 6.0 assists and made his first of three all-star teams. Rose was on his way to stardom; he was considered one of the top three-point guards in the league. In the 2010-11 and 2011-12 season the Bulls won the Central Division led by Rose. He averaged 24.0 and 7.8 assists over that two-year period. He was named MVP in 2011 at the age of 22, the youngest player to ever win the award. In the 2012 playoffs he tore his ACL and for the next two years he played less than 50 games each season. In 2017 he played fewer than 40 games and since 2018 he has dealt with knee issues. In his 12-year career he has been healthy only seven seasons but still has an overall average of 16.2 points and 4.6 assists for his career.

Joel Embiid is an enigma, a mystery, and a head scratcher to anyone, like me, that is trying to pick the best basketball players of all time. There is no question that Embiid has the potential to be an all-time great. However, he has been in the NBA for eight years but did not play a game his first two years due to a foot injury. He played one year in college at the University of Kansas but even in that one year he only averaged 23 minutes a game. He missed the conference tournament and the NCAA tournament due to a back issue. In eight years since he was first drafted in 2014, he has not played in over 61 games in any one season prior to this season. This year he played in 68 games, the most games in a season in his career. He was runner-up in the voting for the MVP. He averaged 30.6 points and 11.4 rebounds. Embiid has a 26 point per game career average and 11.4 rebound average. At 7'0" he is unstoppable offensively and has made the All-Defensive team three times. He has made five All-Star teams and has been picked four times to the All-NBA team. Embiid could be running out of time since he is 28 years old and needs six or seven more productive years to be considered a Top 75 player.

THE YOUNG GUNS

There are several players that are difficult to "classify". Some, like Embiid, are great players but never seem to stay healthy. Others, like Kyrie Erving, miss a lot of games for various other reasons. But there is no denying that when they both play, they are among the best in the game. And then there are the young guys in the league that I call the "Young Guns". These are the guys that are just beginning their journey in the NBA but based on the first few years of their careers they could go on to crack the Top 75 or even become the G.O.A.T. Some of the readers of this book might wonder how I could not include some of these players in my Top 75, right now! By now you have read my criteria and right or wrong I place a lot of importance on longevity. In the case of Luka Doncic his resume is already good enough to be considered one of the best of the best. However, in my opinion, he needs to perform at an elite level for more than 4 or 5 years. For that reason, I am devoting this chapter to those young players that one day when someone sees this book they will not say "How could he have not put so and so on the list. He didn't even mention a particular player just because he was just beginning his career".

The first great young player that has a chance to be in the stratosphere of elite basketball players is the afore mentioned Luka Doncic. Dirk Nowitzki calls Doncic one of the best all-around players that he has ever seen. Since coming into the league in the 2018-19 season he has averaged 26.4 points, 8.0 assists, and 8.5 rebounds a game. In his 3-playoff series he has averaged an unbelievable 32.5 points, 9.3 rebounds, and 7.9 assists per game. Doncic was named to the First Team All-NBA this year for a third time. Nikola Jokic's passing ability is just "insane" said one NBA reporter. He may end up the best passing big man of all time but that's not all he does. At 26 years old he has won 2 MVPs, made the All-NBA team 4 times, and the All-Star team 4 times while averaging 19.7 points, 10.4 rebounds, and 6.2 assists a game. Zion Williamson is a potential top 25 NBA player, but can he stay healthy enough to put together a career is the biggest question mark when talking about this huge man. He has not played a full season since he was drafted #1 overall in 2019. He is only 20 and already has a 25.7 scoring average with a 60% field goal percentage. Zion is an exciting and charismatic player, but he must avoid the injury "bug". Devin Armani Booker at age 25 already has six 20-point seasons. His career average is 23.5 points and 4.7 assists. He made the All-Rookie team as a 19-year-old and has made 3 All-Star appearances. This is the first year that Booker has made First Team All-NBA. Donovan Mitchell has scored at least 20 points per game in all five seasons that he has been in the NBA. Mitchell has a 23.9 career scoring average and 4.5 assists average. He is also an excellent free throw shooter with a .833 average. Jayson Tatum came into the league in the 2017-2018 season and has averaged 20.9 points, and 6.6 rebounds in his five year career. The Celtics have been in the playoffs every year that Tatum has been with them including runner-up to the NBA champion Warriors this past year. His playoff average is almost 23 points a game. He has made 3 All-Star teams and has been named to the All-NBA team twice. Trae Young who some NBA followers refer to as the Steph Curry clone is one of the most exciting of the young guns. He can not only shoot it from "downtown" with his unbelievable range, but he also penetrates and can pass it with the best of them. He is averaging 25.3 points and 9.1 assists for the 4 seasons he has played in the NBA. Young made 3rd Team All-NBA this year. Ja Morant has been compared to Allen Iverson but when I watch him play, I see a smaller version of MJ. He is so explosive and dynamic going to the basket but that could be a liability for him over time because those knocks and bumps take a toll on the body. But right now, he is phenomenal to watch. After two years in the league, he is averaging 21.4 points and 7.1 assists. He has made the All-Star team and this year was named to the 2nd Team All-NBA. Morant was ROY. Karl Anthony Towns is another of the many 'one and doners' that came out of Kentucky. He was drafted #1 in the 2015 draft by the Timberwolves. After 7 years in the NBA, he is averaging 23.2 points and 11.3 rebounds per game. But the most remarkable thing about his offense is that at 6'11" Towns won the 3-point shooting contest and has a .397 3-point field goal percentage. He could become the best big man 3-point shooter in NBA history. He was ROY, a 3-time All-Star selection and has made the All-NBA team twice. At 26 years of age, he is #8 on the active players scoring list and 4th among active players in rebounds per game.

The NBA is in good hands with such great talent as these eight young guns and the other young players such as Giannis, Kawhi, and Damian that are already in my Top 75. Many, if not all these players, will be on the All-Decade team of the 2020s. What do each one of these players have in common besides athleticism? They all started their NBA career at a very young age, some as teenagers. Youth is an athlete's greatest ally and to be able to play in the NBA as young as 18 or 19 years old gives them a great advantage in putting up phenomenal numbers for their career, Top 75 numbers! Ten years or less from now there could be a new name in the top 10 and certainly there will be new additions to the Top 75. I'm not sure there is anyone in the world that is playing basketball right now that can crack the top 5 but in sport never say never.

ACKNOWLEDGEMENTS

I would like to think my beautiful and smart daughters, Amy Crosby and Ashlee Predmore, for editing this book. I want to especially thank my good friend, who contributed enormously with statistics, facts and gems, but has chosen to remain anonymous.

CREDITS:

Basketball-Reference.com
https://www.statmuse.com
https://www.wikipedia.org

About The Author

Jack Sutter fell in love with the game of basketball as an eight-year-old playing on a dirt court in a small town in Southern Illinois. He was the first graduate of Galatia High School to make All-State and earn a basketball scholarship to play in college. He played for three years at Middle Tennessee State University and graduated in 1967.

He taught in the public school system in Detroit, Mi., Salem, Il., and Brandon, Fl. He earned a Master of Arts degree from Eastern Michigan University before joining the basketball staff at Oral Roberts University in

1970. During a four-year tenure from 1970-74 ORU went from an NAIA school to a Division I program. ORU was ranked in the Top 20 and made trips to the NIT in 1972 and 1973.

In 1974 they played in the NCAA Tournament and beat Syracuse and Louisville before losing to Kansas in the finals of the Elite Eight game 93-90 in overtime. From 1969 to 1974 ORU won 118 games and lost only 23. They led the nation in scoring three of those five years, averaging over 90 points. Sutter has coached for 22 years at the D1 level, junior college, and high school level. He has played against and coached several players who have played in the NBA.

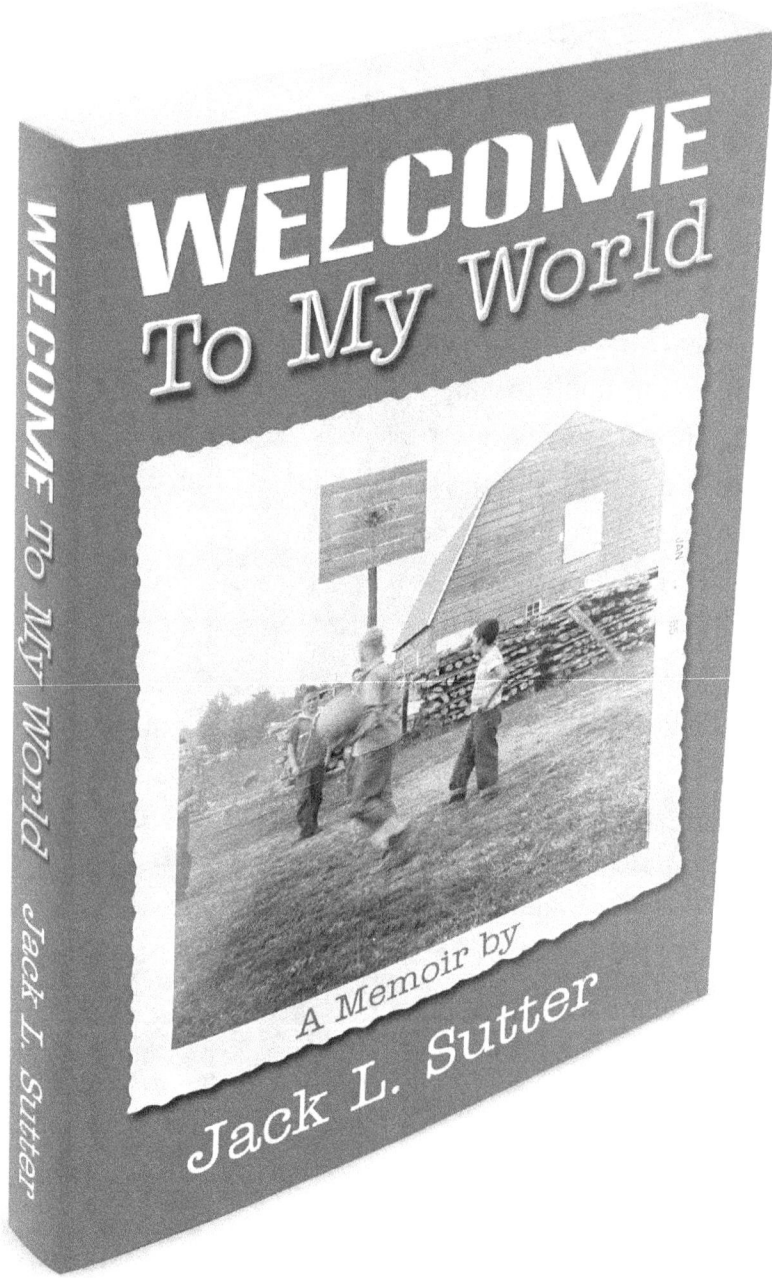

JackoMaxo1@gmail.com
Social Media – JackoMaxo1